GENERATION X CAREGIVERS

Thrive Using Person-Centered Care with Aging Parents

MICHAEL T. LATTIMORE

The information contained in this book is based on the author's research, personal experiences, and interviews with experts in the field.
Any trademarks, service marks, product names, or named features mentioned in this book are assumed to be the property of their respective owners and are used only for reference.

The author and publisher disclaim any liability, loss, or risk incurred as a direct or indirect consequence of the use and application of any of the contents of this book. The reader is solely responsible for their own actions and decisions.

Michael T. Lattimore michael@mpulsehomecare.com

Printed Worldwide
First Printing 2024
First Edition 2024

ISBN: 979-8-9898438-3-1

10 9 8 7 6 5 4 3 2 1

Cover design by Michael Lattimore
For information regarding bulk purchases, please contact: Michael Lattimore,
Founder and CEO
Published by: MPULSE LLC
3540 Toringdon Way
Suite 200 #1137
Charlotte, NC 28277
1-855-799-1015

"I want to thank my brother Eric and parents Abe and Elizabeth Lattimore for your unwavering love and support."
"To my legacy Matthias and Malahkai, you are my inspiration, and I will love you both forever."

TABLE OF CONTENTS

This table of contents includes a dedicated section on non-emergency medical transportation (NEMT) services within the "Navigating Healthcare Systems and Resources" chapter. This section highlights the importance of reliable transportation for medical appointments, provides information on accessing NEMT services for aging parents, and discusses the benefits of utilizing NEMT for their healthcare needs.

By including NEMT information, the comprehensive guide acknowledges the role of transportation services in ensuring that aging parents can access necessary medical care and appointments. It provides caregivers with valuable insights into the benefits and availability of NEMT services, further enhancing the support provided by MPULSE NEMT Homecare.

FOREWORD

In the realm of caregiving literature, there are books that touch the surface, and then there are those that delve deep into the heart of the matter, leaving an indelible mark on the reader's soul. "Generation X Caregivers: Thrive Using Person-Centered Care with Aging Parents" undoubtedly belongs to the latter category. It is my first work that transcends the boundaries of a mere guidebook, offering a profound exploration of the challenges faced by Generation X caregivers and providing them with the tools and wisdom they need to navigate their unique journey.

From the moment you delve into the pages of this comprehensive guide, my unwavering commitment is to person-centered care. Hopefully my voice resonates with authenticity, drawing readers into a world where aging parents are not just recipients of care, but individuals deserving of respect, dignity, and personalized support. With each turn of the page, I try to illuminate the path for caregivers who often find themselves overwhelmed and uncertain.

What sets my book apart is its unwavering dedication to empowering Generation X caregivers. It goes beyond surface-level advice and delves into the emotional, psychological, and practical aspects of caregiving. I understand the unique challenges faced by this generation and can skillfully navigate the complexities of balancing their own lives while providing the utmost care for their aging parents.

This goal of this book is to offer solace to those who may feel isolated in their caregiving journey. It serves as a guiding light, illuminating the path towards person-centered care that not only enhances the lives of aging parents but also nurtures the wellbeing of caregivers themselves. My insights, backed by extensive research and personal experiences, provide a roadmap for creating a nurturing environment that fosters connection, compassion, and joy.

To the Generation X caregivers who may feel overwhelmed, exhausted, or uncertain, I implore you to embrace the wisdom within these pages. Allow yourself to be guided by my expertise, compassion, and unwavering belief in the power of person-centered care. Through this book, you will find the strength to navigate the challenges, the inspiration to create meaningful connections, and the tools to provide the best possible support for your aging parents.

To the readers who may not be caregivers themselves, I urge you to explore the depths of this book's message. It is a call to action, a reminder that we all have a role to play in supporting and uplifting those who care for our aging loved ones. By understanding the unique struggles faced by Generation X caregivers and embracing the principles of person-centered care, we collectively create a society that values and cherishes our elders.

Michael T. Lattimore,
Specialized NEMT Homecare Entrepreneur and Consultant
Certified Environmental Access Consultant (C.E.A.C)
Program of All-Inclusive Care for the Elderly provider (PACE)
Former NFL Defensive End – New Orleans Saints

CHAPTER 1

Introduction

I am thrilled to introduce you to 'Generation X Caregivers: Thrive Using Person-Centered Care with Aging Parents,' a groundbreaking book that addresses the pressing challenges faced by Generation X caregivers like me and countless others in the healthcare industry. As a healthcare entrepreneur with 20 years of non-emergency medical transportation (NEMT) ownership experience in transporting clients to medical appointments, hospital discharges, dialysis, and surgeries, I bring a unique perspective to the forefront, shedding light on a critical issue that often goes unnoticed.

In this comprehensive guide, I delve into the heart of the matter – the plight of aging parents living home alone and the lack of support they encounter. Drawing from my vast knowledge and data as a specialized NEMT entrepreneur, Program of All-Inclusive Care for the Elderly (PACE) transportation provider, and a VGM Live Certified Environment Access Consultant (C.E.A.C), I paint a vivid picture of the struggles faced by these individuals, particularly when they have multiple steps at their residence, making the situation even more challenging.

As a seasoned healthcare expert, I understand the profound impact this predicament has on both the aging parents and their children, like me, who may live in another state or have demanding work schedules. I recognize that most of us find ourselves at a loss, unsure of how to provide the necessary assistance and care our parents require. This knowledge fuels my mission to empower and educate Generation X caregivers, equipping us with the tools and strategies needed to navigate this complex landscape.

Through my book, I aim to bridge the gap between caregivers and aging parents, offering practical solutions and guidance to ensure a smooth transition to aging gracefully at home. By addressing the challenges faced by these vulnerable individuals, I seek to prevent hospital readmissions and promote the overall wellbeing of aging parents.

'Generation X Caregivers: Thrive Using Person-Centered Care with Aging Parents' is not just a book; it is a call to action. My compelling and detailed insights serve as a catalyst for change, urging healthcare professionals, caregivers, and society to recognize the importance of person- centered care for aging parents. With my expertise and compassionate approach, I provide a roadmap for success, enabling caregivers like us to create nurturing and supportive environments that promote independence, dignity, and overall well-being.

Prepare to embark on a transformative journey as 'Generation X Caregivers: Thrive Using Person-Centered Care with Aging Parents' revolutionizes the way we approach caregiving, ensuring that no aging parent is left alone and vulnerable after hospital discharges or surgeries. Let me be your guide as I empower you to make a difference in the lives of those who need it most. Together, we can create a brighter future for our aging parents and ourselves.

Generation X caregivers face unique challenges and responsibilities in caring for their aging parents. Balancing the demands of their careers, their own families, and caregiving can be overwhelming, leading to feelings of guilt, stress, and burnout. However, by prioritizing self- care, setting boundaries, and seeking support, Generation X caregivers can navigate these challenges more effectively.

Financial considerations also pose a significant challenge for Generation X caregivers, as they strive to establish financial stability while managing the costs of caregiving. Open communication with employers, exploring flexible work arrangements, and seeking financial assistance or resources can help alleviate some of the financial burden.

The emotional impact of caregiving should not be overlooked. Witnessing the decline of their parents' health and independence, as well as the role reversal of becoming the nurturer, can evoke complex emotions. Generation X caregivers should acknowledge and address their emotions, seeking support from others and practicing self-compassion. Taking breaks, engaging in self-care activities, and seeking professional counseling or therapy can help caregivers manage the emotional challenges of caregiving.

Through this comprehensive guide, I aim to empower and educate caregivers, equipping them with the tools and strategies needed to navigate the complex landscape of caregiving. By bridging the gap between caregivers and aging parents, I offer practical solutions and guidance to ensure a smooth transition to aging gracefully at home.

This book serves as a call to action, urging healthcare professionals, caregivers, and society to recognize the importance of person-centered care for aging parents. By promoting independence, dignity, and overall well-being, we can prevent hospital readmissions and create nurturing and supportive environments for our aging parents.

I invite you to join me on this transformative journey as we revolutionize the way we approach caregiving. Together, we can make a difference in the lives of those who need it most and create a brighter future for our aging parents and ourselves. Let 'Generation X Caregivers: Thrive Using Person-Centered Care with Aging Parents' be your guide as we navigate the challenges of caregiving and ensure that no aging parent is left alone and vulnerable.

In conclusion, 'Generation X Caregivers: Thrive Using Person-Centered Care with Aging Parents' is a groundbreaking book that addresses the pressing challenges faced by Generation X caregivers in providing care for their aging parents.

With my expertise and unique perspective as a healthcare expert, I shed light on the struggles faced by aging parents living home alone and the lack of support they encounter.

FAQS – CHAPTER 1

Understanding Person-Centered Care

- What is person-centered care, and why is it important for aging parents?
- How can person-centered care improve the quality of life for my parents?
- What are the key principles and benefits of person-centered care?
- What is person-centered care, and why is it important for aging parents?

Person-centered care is an approach to healthcare that prioritizes the individual's preferences, values, and needs. It recognizes that each person is unique and should be actively involved in their own care decisions. For aging parents, person-centered care is crucial as it promotes dignity, autonomy, and respect. It ensures that their individual goals, preferences, and values are considered in all aspects of their care, leading to a more personalized and meaningful experience.

How can person-centered care improve the quality of life for my parents?

Person-centered care can significantly improve the quality of life for aging parents in several ways:

1. Enhanced autonomy and control: By involving your parents in care decisions, person-centered care empowers them to have a say in their own lives, fostering a sense of control and independence.

2. Improved communication and trust: Person-centered care encourages open and honest communication between healthcare providers, caregivers, and your parents. This trust-based relationship can lead to better understanding, shared decision-making, and improved overall care outcomes.

3. Tailored care and support: By considering your parents' unique preferences, values, and needs, person-centered care ensures that their care plan is personalized and aligned with their goals. This can lead to more effective and targeted interventions, resulting in improved physical, emotional, and social well-being.

4. Increased satisfaction and engagement: When your parents feel heard, respected, and involved in their care, they are more likely to be satisfied with their healthcare experience. This can contribute to a greater sense of engagement and overall satisfaction with life.

What are the key principles and benefits of person-centered care?

The key principles of person-centered care include:

1. Respect for individual preferences and values.
2. Collaboration and shared decision-making between healthcare providers, caregivers, and your parents.
3. Recognition of the individual's unique needs and circumstances.
4. Continuity and coordination of care across different healthcare settings.

The benefits of person-centered care include:

1. Improved health outcomes: Person-centered care has been associated with better health outcomes, including improved medication adherence, reduced hospitalizations, and enhanced overall well-being.
2. Increased satisfaction: By prioritizing your parents' preferences and involving them in care decisions, person-centered care can lead to higher levels of satisfaction with their healthcare experience.
3. Enhanced caregiver engagement: Person-centered care recognizes the importance of involving caregivers in the care process. By valuing their input and involving them in decision-making, person-centered care can improve caregiver engagement and satisfaction.

4. Better communication and understanding: Person-centered care promote effective communication between healthcare providers, caregivers, and your parents. This can lead to a better understanding of your parents' needs, preferences, and goals, resulting in more tailored and effective care.

5. Increased dignity and respect: Person-centered care places a strong emphasis on treating your parents with dignity and respect. This can help maintain their sense of identity, autonomy, and self-worth, leading to a higher quality of life.

6. Improved overall experience: By focusing on the individual and their unique needs, person- centered care aims to provide a more positive and meaningful healthcare experience for your parents. This can contribute to a sense of well-being, satisfaction, and improved overall quality of life.

It's important to note that person-centered care is a collaborative effort between healthcare providers, caregivers, and your parents. By working together and prioritizing the individual's needs and preferences, person-centered care can have a significant positive impact on the well- being and quality of life of aging parents.

CHAPTER 2

The Role of Generation X Caregivers

Challenges and Responsibilities of Generation X Caregivers

Caring for aging parents is a responsibility that falls heavily on the shoulders of Generation X individuals. Born between the early 1960s and early 1980s, Generation X finds themselves in a unique position, sandwiched between the demands of their own families and the increasing needs of their aging parents. This generation faces a set of challenges and responsibilities that are distinct from those of previous generations.

One of the primary challenges faced by Generation X caregivers is the sheer magnitude of the caregiving role. Many individuals in this generation are not only caring for their aging parents but also raising their own children. This dual responsibility can be overwhelming, as it requires balancing the needs of multiple generations simultaneously. Generation X caregivers often find themselves juggling work, family, and caregiving responsibilities, leaving little time for self-care and personal pursuits.

Financial considerations also pose a significant challenge for Generation X caregivers. Many individuals in this generation are still in the midst of their careers, striving to establish financial stability and save for their own retirement. However, the cost of caregiving can be substantial, including expenses related to medical care, home modifications, and long-term care services. Balancing the financial demands of caregiving with their own financial goals can be a daunting task for Generation X caregivers.

Balancing Multiple Roles: Career, Family, and Caregiving

Generation X caregivers often find themselves caught in the middle, trying to balance the demands of their careers, their own families, and the needs of their aging parents. This delicate balancing act can lead to feelings of guilt, stress, and burnout. The pressure to excel in their careers while also providing quality care for their parents can be overwhelming.

To navigate this challenge, Generation X caregivers must prioritize and set boundaries. It is essential to communicate openly with employers about the caregiving responsibilities and explore flexible work arrangements, such as remote work or flexible hours. Seeking support from family members, friends, and community resources can also help alleviate some of the caregiving burden. Delegating tasks and responsibilities to others can provide much needed relief and create a support network for both the caregiver and the aging parent.

Self-care is another crucial aspect of balancing multiple roles. Generation X caregivers must prioritize their own physical, emotional, and mental well-being. Taking time for self-care activities, such as exercise, hobbies, and relaxation, is not selfish but essential for maintaining their own health and resilience.

By prioritizing self-care, Generation X caregivers can recharge and better meet the demands of their caregiving responsibilities.

The Emotional Impact of Caregiving

Caring for aging parents can have a profound emotional impact on Generation X caregivers. Witnessing the decline of their parents' health and independence can be emotionally challenging and may evoke feelings of sadness, grief, and loss. The role reversal, where the caregiver becomes the nurturer, can also be emotionally complex and may trigger feelings of guilt or resentment.

Moreover, the constant demands of caregiving can lead to caregiver burnout and emotional exhaustion. The physical and emotional toll of providing care, coupled with the pressures of balancing multiple roles, can leave Generation X caregivers feeling overwhelmed and emotionally drained.

It is crucial for Generation X caregivers to acknowledge and address their emotions. Seeking support from friends, family, or support groups can provide a safe space to share feelings and experiences. Professional counseling or therapy can also be beneficial in navigating the emotional challenges of caregiving. Taking breaks and practicing self-care activities that promote emotional well-being, such as meditation, journaling, or engaging in hobbies, can help caregivers manage stress and maintain emotional resilience.

In addition, it is important for Generation X caregivers to recognize the importance of self- compassion. Caregiving is a demanding role, and it is natural to experience a range of emotions.

Being kind to oneself, practicing self-acceptance, and acknowledging personal limitations can help alleviate feelings of guilt or inadequacy.

By acknowledging and addressing the emotional impact of caregiving, Generation X caregivers can better support their own well-being and provide more compassionate care for their aging parents.

Generation X caregivers face unique challenges and responsibilities in caring for their aging parents. Balancing the demands of their careers, their own families, and caregiving can be overwhelming, leading to feelings of guilt, stress, and burnout. However, by prioritizing self- care, setting boundaries, and seeking support, Generation X caregivers can navigate these challenges more effectively.

Financial considerations also pose a significant challenge for Generation X caregivers, as they strive to establish financial stability while managing the costs of caregiving. Open communication with employers, exploring flexible work arrangements, and seeking financial assistance or resources can help alleviate some of the financial burden.

The emotional impact of caregiving should not be overlooked. Witnessing the decline of their parents' health and independence, as well as the role reversal of becoming the nurturer, can evoke complex emotions. Generation X caregivers should acknowledge and address their emotions, seeking support from others and practicing self-compassion.

Taking breaks, engaging in self-care activities, and seeking professional counseling or therapy can help caregivers manage the emotional challenges of caregiving.

In conclusion, Generation X caregivers play a vital role in caring for their aging parents. By prioritizing self-care, seeking support, and addressing the emotional impact of caregiving, they can provide compassionate care while maintaining their own wellbeing. Let us continue to advocate for resources and support systems that recognize and address the unique challenges faced by Generation X caregivers, ensuring that they receive the support they need to navigate this important role.

FAQS - CHAPTER 2

The Role of Generation X Caregivers

How can I build a strong relationship with my parents' healthcare team?

Building a strong relationship with your parents' healthcare team is essential for effective communication and collaboration. Here are some tips:

1. Establish open lines of communication: Introduce yourself and express your commitment to being involved in your parents' care. Ask for the best way to communicate with the healthcare team and provide your contact information.

2. Be proactive and prepared: Come prepared with a list of questions or concerns for each appointment. Take notes during discussions and ask for clarification if needed.

3. Show respect and appreciation: Treat the healthcare team with respect and acknowledge their expertise. Express gratitude for their efforts and the care they provide.

4. Foster a collaborative approach: Share information about your parents' medical history, medications, and any changes in their condition. Offer insights into their preferences, values, and goals to help guide the care plan.

5. Follow through and communicate updates: Keep the healthcare team informed about any changes in your parents' condition, medications, or treatments. Follow up on recommendations or referrals and provide feedback on the effectiveness of interventions.

What are some tips for effective communication with doctors, nurses, and therapists?

Effective communication with healthcare professionals is crucial for ensuring the best care for your parents. Here are some tips:

1. Be clear and concise: Clearly articulate your concerns or questions using simple and straightforward language. Avoid medical jargon and ask for explanations if something is unclear.

2. Actively listen: Pay attention to what the healthcare professional is saying and ask for clarification if needed. Take notes to help you remember important information.

3. Ask questions: Don't hesitate to ask questions to gain a better understanding of your parents' condition, treatment options, or potential side effects. This will help you make informed decisions.

4. Share information: Provide relevant information about your parents' medical history, symptoms, and any changes in their condition. This will help the healthcare professional make accurate assessments and recommendations.

5. Seek clarification on treatment plans: Make sure you understand the recommended treatment plan, including medications, therapies, or lifestyle changes. Ask about potential risks, benefits, and alternatives.

6. Request written instructions: Ask for written instructions or summaries of the visit, including any changes to medications or treatments. This will help you remember and follow through on the recommendations.

How can I ensure that my voice is heard and that my parents' needs and preferences are considered in decision-making processes?

Ensuring that your voice is heard, and your parents' needs and preferences are considered in decision-making processes requires active engagement and advocacy. Here are some strategies to help:

1. Be an active participant: Actively engage in discussions and decision-making processes. Share your insights, concerns, and preferences regarding your parents' care.

2. Establish a partnership: Build a collaborative relationship with the healthcare team. Emphasize that you are a valuable member of the care team and that your input is essential for making informed decisions.

3. Communicate clearly and assertively: Clearly express your parents' needs, preferences, and goals. Use "I" statements to convey your perspective and assertively advocate for their best interests.

4. Ask for clarification: If you don't understand something or need more information, don't hesitate to ask for clarification. Request additional explanations or examples to ensure a clear understanding.

5. Request shared decision-making: Advocate for shared decision-making, where the healthcare team and your family work together to make decisions. This involves considering the benefits, risks, and alternatives of different treatment options. Seek a second opinion if necessary: If you have concerns or doubts about a recommended treatment or diagnosis, don't hesitate to seek a second opinion from another healthcare professional. This can provide additional perspectives and options.

6. Document and organize information: Keep a record of important information, including test results, treatment plans, and discussions with healthcare professionals. This will help you stay organized and refer back to information when needed.

7. Utilize patient advocacy resources: Familiarize yourself with patient advocacy resources and organizations that can provide guidance and support. They can offer advice on navigating the healthcare system and help ensure your voice is heard.

Remember, effective communication and advocacy are key to ensuring that your parents' needs and preferences are considered in decision-making processes. By actively engaging with the healthcare team and advocating for your parents, you can help shape their care plan and ensure the best possible outcomes.

CHAPTER 3

Effective Communication and Collaboration

Building Strong Relationships with Healthcare Teams

As Generation X caregivers navigate the complex healthcare system on behalf of their aging parents, building strong relationships with healthcare teams becomes paramount. Effective communication and collaboration with doctors, nurses, therapists, and other healthcare professionals are essential for ensuring the best possible care for aging parents.

To build strong relationships with healthcare teams, Generation X caregivers should prioritize open and honest communication. This involves actively listening to healthcare professionals, asking questions, and seeking clarification when needed. By demonstrating a genuine interest in understanding their loved one's medical condition and treatment options, caregivers can establish trust and foster collaborative relationships with healthcare providers.

Additionally, caregivers should strive to be proactive and well-informed advocates for their aging parents. This includes staying up to date on their loved one's medical history, medications, and treatment plans.

By actively participating in care discussions and sharing relevant information with healthcare teams, caregivers can contribute valuable insights and ensure that their loved one's needs are met.

Communicating Effectively with Doctors, Nurses, and Therapists

Effective communication with doctors, nurses, and therapists is crucial for Generation X caregivers to navigate the healthcare system and advocate for their aging parents. Clear and concise communication ensures that important information is conveyed accurately, and that caregivers' concerns are addressed.

When communicating with healthcare professionals, caregivers should come prepared with a list of questions or concerns. This helps ensure that all relevant topics are discussed during appointments or consultations. Caregivers should also take notes during these interactions to ensure that they have a record of important information and instructions.

It is important for caregivers to speak up and ask for clarification if they do not understand something. Healthcare professionals can sometimes use medical jargon or complex terminology, which may be unfamiliar to caregivers. By seeking clarification, caregivers can ensure that they have a clear understanding of their loved one's condition, treatment options, and any necessary follow-up care.

In addition to verbal communication, caregivers should also utilize written communication tools to enhance their interactions with healthcare teams. This can include maintaining a comprehensive medical history and medication list, as well as documenting any changes or updates in their loved one's condition. Sharing this information with healthcare professionals helps ensure continuity of care and reduces the risk of medical errors.

Involving Caregivers in Decision-Making Processes

Caregivers play a vital role in the care and well-being of their aging parents, and their input should be valued and respected in the decision-making processes. Generation X caregivers should actively seek opportunities to be involved in discussions and decisions regarding their loved one's care.

To effectively participate in decision-making processes, caregivers should educate themselves about their loved one's medical condition, treatment options, and potential risks and benefits. This knowledge empowers caregivers to ask informed questions and contributes to the decision- making process from a place of understanding.

Caregivers should also express their preferences and concerns to healthcare teams. By openly sharing their perspectives, caregivers can ensure that their loved one's care aligns with their values and goals. This may involve discussing treatment options, exploring alternative therapies, or advocating for specific interventions or services.

Involving caregivers in decision-making processes also requires healthcare professionals to recognize and respect their expertise and insights. Caregivers often have a deep understanding of their loved one's needs, preferences, and daily routines. By valuing and incorporating this knowledge into care plans, healthcare teams can provide more person-centered and effective care.

Furthermore, caregivers should actively seek opportunities to collaborate with healthcare teams. This can involve attending care conferences, participating in care planning meetings, or engaging in shared decision-making discussions. By actively participating in these collaborative processes, caregivers can contribute their unique perspectives and ensure that their loved one's care is comprehensive and holistic.

Effective communication and collaboration with healthcare teams are crucial for Generation X caregivers to navigate the complex healthcare system and advocate for their aging parents. By building strong relationships, communicating effectively, and actively participating in decision- making processes, caregivers can ensure that their loved ones receive the best possible care.

Open and honest communication, active listening, and asking questions are essential for establishing trust and fostering collaborative relationships with healthcare professionals. Caregivers should come prepared with questions and concerns, take notes during appointments, and seek clarification when needed. Utilizing written communication tools, such as maintaining a comprehensive medical history and medication list, enhances interactions with healthcare teams and ensures continuity of care.

Caregivers should also be actively involved in decision-making processes, educating themselves about their loved one's condition and treatment options. By expressing their preferences and concerns, caregivers can ensure that care aligns with their values and goals. Healthcare professionals should recognize and respect caregivers' expertise and insights, valuing their knowledge of their loved one's needs and routines.

Active collaboration with healthcare teams, such as attending care conferences and participating in shared decision-making discussions, allows caregivers to contribute their unique perspectives and ensure comprehensive and holistic care.

In conclusion, effective communication and collaboration with healthcare teams empower Generation X caregivers to advocate for their aging parents and ensure the best possible care. By prioritizing open communication, actively participating in decision-making, and collaborating with healthcare professionals, caregivers can navigate the healthcare system with confidence and provide the highest quality of care for their loved ones.

FAQS - CHAPTER 3

Effective Communication and Collaboration

You must collaborate with your entire healthcare team. Here are some practical tips:

Q1: How can I initiate effective communication with my parents' health care team?

A1: *Start by introducing yourself as a committed partner in your parents' care. Inquire about the preferred communication methods of the healthcare team and provide your contact information.*

Q2: What steps can I take to be more proactive and prepared for healthcare appointments?

A2: *Come prepared with a comprehensive list of your parents' medical history and develop a set of questions or concerns before appointments. Actively participate in discussions and take notes for further reference.*

Q3: How should I express respect and appreciation to the health care team?

A3: *Acknowledge the expertise of each team member, using inclusive language that values both health care professionals and family members. Regularly express gratitude for their dedication and efforts in providing care.*

Q4: What role does collaboration play in my parents' care?

A4: *Foster a collaborative approach by sharing information about your parents' medical history, preferences, and values. Encourage open dialogue, ask for teams' input on decisions, and actively listen to their recommendations.*

Q5: How can I keep the health care team informed about changes in my parents' condition?

A5: Establish regular communication channels and provide updates on any changes in your parents' conditions, medications, or treatments. Follow through on recommendations and share feedback on the effectiveness of interventions.

Q6: Why is it important to humanize my parents' healthcare experience?

A6: By sharing information about your parents' life, interests, and preferences, you contribute to a person-centered care approach. This helps the health care team tailor their care plan to align with your parents' unique identity.

Q7: What should I do if there are changes in the care plan or treatment recommendations?

A7: Act promptly on recommendations or referrals and communicate outcomes or challenges experience. Provide constructive feedback on the effectiveness of interventions to ensure continuous improvement in care.

Q8: How can I emphasize the importance of shared decision making and the health care process?

A8: Encourage open dialogue, ask for the healthcare team's input on decisions, and actively involve them in the decision-making process.

Q9: How can I ensure that my parents healthcare team understands their lifestyle and preferences?

A9: Actively communicate your parents lifestyle choices, hobbies, and preferences during discussions. This helps the healthcare team incorporate these aspects into the care plan.

Q10: *What steps can I take to contribute to ongoing improvements in my parents' care?*

A10: Stay informed about the latest developments in your parents' health, provide timely updates to the healthcare team, and actively participate in care plan reviews to contribute to continuous improvement.

Q11: *How do I navigate complex medical information and ensure clarity in communication?*

A11: Request explanations in playing language, ask for visual aids or written summaries, and seek clarification on any medical jargon or complex information to ensure a clear understanding.

Q12: *What role does trust play in building a strong relationship with the healthcare team?*

A12: Trust is essential. Building trust through open communication, consistency, and actively engaging with the health care team. Trust fosters a positive and collaborative environment.

Q13: *How can I involve other family members in the collaborative care process?*

A13: Facilitate family discussions about your parents' care, share updates, and encourage other family members to participate in healthcare appointments to ensure a collective and informed approach.

Q14: *Are there resources available to help me better understand my parents' medical conditions and treatment options?*

A14: Ask the health care team for educational resources, attend support groups, and explore reputable online sources to enhance your understanding of your parents' medical conditions and treatment options.

Q15: What should I do if there is a disagreement with the health care team about my parents' care?

A15: initiate open and respectful discussions to address concerns, seek additional opinions if necessary, and work collaboratively to find a solution to that aligns with your parents' best interests.

Q16: How can I ensure continuity of care during transitions, such as hospital discharge or changes in healthcare providers?

A16: Communicate proactively during transitions, share relevant medical records, and ensure that the incoming healthcare team is well informed about your parents' history, preferences, and ongoing care needs.

Q17: What role does self-care play for family members and the health care journey?

A17: Prioritize self-care to maintain your own well-being. This ensures you are better equipped to support your parents and collaborate effectively with the healthcare team over the long term.

CHAPTER 4

Understanding and Meeting the Unique Needs of Aging Parents

Conducting a Comprehensive Assessment of Needs and Preferences

To provide the best possible care for aging parents, Generation X caregivers must first conduct a comprehensive assessment of their loved one's needs and preferences. This assessment serves as the foundation for developing a personalized care plan that addresses their unique requirements.

The assessment should encompass various aspects of their loved one's life, including physical health, mental well-being, social connections, and daily activities. Caregivers should consider factors such as medical conditions, medication management, mobility challenges, cognitive abilities, emotional needs, and social support systems. By gathering this information, caregivers can gain a holistic understanding of their loved one's current situation and identify areas where additional support may be required.

Addressing Medical Conditions and Mobility Challenges

As aging parents face medical conditions and mobility challenges, it is crucial for Generation X caregivers to address these issues effectively. This involves working closely with healthcare professionals to manage chronic illnesses, monitor medications, and ensure regular medical check-ups.

Caregivers should also focus on creating a safe and accessible living environment for their aging parents. This may involve making home modifications, such as installing grab bars in bathrooms, removing tripping hazards, or arranging for assistive devices like walkers or wheelchairs. By addressing mobility challenges, caregivers can enhance their loved one's safety and independence.

Regular exercise and physical therapy can also play a vital role in maintaining and improving mobility for aging parents. Caregivers should work with healthcare professionals to develop appropriate exercise routines and ensure that their loved ones have access to necessary therapy services.

Cultural Considerations and Religious Preferences

Understanding and respecting the cultural considerations and religious preferences of aging parents is essential for Generation X caregivers. Cultural and religious beliefs can significantly impact their loved one's care and well-being.

Caregivers should engage in open and respectful conversations with their aging parents about their cultural and religious beliefs. This includes understanding their preferences for healthcare providers, treatment options, end-of-life care, and rituals or practices that hold significance to them. By incorporating these preferences into the care plan, caregivers can ensure that their loved ones' cultural and religious needs are respected and honored.

Nutrition and Dietary Considerations for Aging Parents

Proper nutrition and dietary considerations are crucial for maintaining the health and well- being of aging parents. Generation X caregivers should pay close attention to their loved one's nutritional needs and work with healthcare professionals to develop a balanced dietary plan.

Caregivers should consider any dietary restrictions or allergies their aging parents may have and ensure that meals are tailored to meet their specific needs. This may involve consulting with a nutritionist or dietitian to create a meal plan that provides adequate nutrients while accommodating any dietary restrictions.

In addition to addressing specific dietary needs, caregivers should also promote healthy eating habits for their aging parents. This includes encouraging the consumption of fruits, vegetables, whole grains, and lean proteins, while limiting the intake of processed foods, sugary snacks, and excessive sodium. Caregivers can play an active role in meal planning, grocery shopping, and meal preparation to ensure that their loved ones have access to nutritious and balanced meals.

Furthermore, hydration is a critical aspect of maintaining overall health for aging parents. Caregivers should ensure that their loved ones are drinking enough fluids throughout the day, as dehydration can lead to various health complications. Offering water, herbal teas, and other hydrating beverages can help promote proper hydration.

It is important for caregivers to be mindful of any changes in their loved one's appetite or dietary preferences. Aging parents may experience changes in taste, appetite, or difficulty chewing or swallowing, which can impact their nutritional intake. In such cases, caregivers should consult with healthcare professionals to explore alternative options, such as pureed or soft foods, to ensure that their loved ones are receiving adequate nutrition.

Understanding and meeting the unique needs of aging parents is a crucial responsibility for Generation X caregivers. By conducting a comprehensive assessment of their loved one's needs and preferences, caregivers can develop personalized care plans that address their unique requirements.

Addressing medical conditions and mobility challenges is essential for ensuring the health and safety of aging parents. Working closely with healthcare professionals, caregivers can manage chronic illnesses, monitor medications, and create a safe and accessible living environment.

Regular exercise and physical therapy can also play a vital role in maintaining and improving mobility.

Cultural considerations and religious preferences should be respected and incorporated into the care plan. Engaging in open and respectful conversations about cultural and religious beliefs allows caregivers to honor their loved ones' preferences and ensure that their care aligns with their values.

Proper nutrition and dietary considerations are crucial for maintaining the health and well- being of aging parents. Caregivers should work with healthcare professionals to develop balanced meal plans that meet their loved ones' specific needs and promote healthy eating habits. Hydration should also be prioritized, and caregivers should be mindful of any changes in appetite or dietary preferences.

In conclusion, by understanding and meeting the unique needs of aging parents, Generation X caregivers can provide the best possible care and support. By addressing medical conditions, mobility challenges, cultural considerations, and dietary needs, caregivers can enhance their loved ones' quality of life and ensure their well-being.

FAQS - CHAPTER 4

Understanding and Meeting the Unique Needs of Aging Parents

How can I conduct a comprehensive assessment of my parents' needs and preferences?

Conducting a comprehensive assessment of your parents' needs and preferences involves gathering information about their physical, emotional, social, and cognitive well-being. Here are some strategies:

1. Communicate openly: Have open and honest conversations with your parents about their current health, any symptoms or concerns they may have, and their goals and preferences for their care.

2. Consult healthcare professionals: Seek input from healthcare professionals who are familiar with your parents' medical history and conditions. They can provide valuable insights and assessments.

3. Observe daily activities: Observe how your parents manage their daily activities, such as personal care, mobility, and household tasks. This can help identify areas where they may need assistance or adaptations.

4. Involve other caregivers: If there are other caregivers involved, such as siblings or other family members, collaborate with them to gather information and perspectives on your parents' needs and preferences.

5. Consider cultural and religious factors: Take into account your parents' cultural and religious beliefs, as these can influence their preferences for care and decision-making.

What are some strategies for addressing medical conditions and mobility challenges?

Addressing medical conditions and mobility challenges requires a comprehensive approach. Here are some strategies:

1. Consult healthcare professionals: Work closely with healthcare professionals to understand your parents' medical conditions, treatment options, and management strategies.

2. Ensure medication management: Help your parents organize and manage their medications, ensuring they take them as prescribed and attend medical appointments regularly.

3. Assistive devices and home modifications: Consider assistive devices such as walkers, canes, or grab bars to enhance mobility and safety at home. Explore home modifications to accommodate any physical limitations.

4. Physical therapy and exercise: Encourage your parents to engage in physical therapy or exercise programs tailored to their abilities and medical conditions. This can help improve mobility, strength, and overall well-being.

5. Fall prevention: Take steps to minimize fall risks by removing hazards, improving lighting, and encouraging regular eye exams. Consider installing safety features like handrails or non-slip mats.

6. Seek professional help: If needed, consult with healthcare professionals specializing in geriatric care or rehabilitation to develop personalized strategies for addressing specific medical conditions and mobility challenges.

How can I respect and accommodate my parents' cultural and religious preferences?

Respecting and accommodating your parents' cultural and religious preferences is important for their overall well-being and sense of identity. Here are some strategies to consider:

1. Open and respectful communication: Have open and respectful conversations with your parents about their cultural and religious beliefs, values, and practices. Listen actively and seek to understand their perspectives.

2. Educate yourself: Take the time to learn about your parents' cultural and religious background. This will help you better understand their preferences and needs.

3. Involve community and religious leaders: Engage community and religious leaders who can provide guidance and support in honoring your parents' cultural and religious preferences. They can offer insights and resources to help you navigate specific situations.

4. Accommodate rituals and practices: Make efforts to accommodate and respect your parents' rituals and practices within the constraints of their health and safety. This may involve adjusting schedules, providing appropriate spaces, or arranging for religious or cultural services.

5. Seek culturally sensitive healthcare: When seeking healthcare services, consider providers who are culturally sensitive and understand the importance of respecting cultural and religious preferences. They can help ensure that your parents' beliefs and practices are considered in their care.

What are some important considerations regarding nutrition and dietary needs for aging parents?

Nutrition and dietary needs play a crucial role in the health and well-being of aging parents. Here are some important considerations:

1. Balanced and varied diet: Encourage your parents to consume a balanced and varied diet that includes fruits, vegetables, whole grains, lean proteins, and healthy fats. This can help provide essential nutrients and support overall health.

2. Adequate hydration: Ensure that your parents are drinking enough fluids throughout the day to stay hydrated. Offer water, herbal teas, or other hydrating beverages.

3. Special dietary needs: Consider any special dietary needs or restrictions your parents may have, such as food allergies, intolerances, or medical conditions like diabetes or hypertension. Consult with healthcare professionals or a registered dietitian for guidance on appropriate dietary modifications.

4. Meal planning and preparation: Assist your parents with meal planning and preparation, considering their preferences, cultural or religious dietary restrictions, and any physical limitations they may have.

5. Regular nutrition assessments: Schedule regular nutrition assessments with healthcare professionals or registered dietitians to monitor your parents' nutritional status and address any deficiencies or concerns.

6. Consider supplements: In consultation with healthcare professionals, consider the need for supplements to address any nutrient deficiencies that cannot be met through diet alone.

Remember, it's important to involve your parents in discussions and decision-making regarding their nutrition and dietary needs. Respect their preferences and cultural considerations while ensuring that their nutritional requirements are met. Consulting with healthcare professionals or registered dietitians can provide valuable guidance and support in addressing specific dietary needs and concerns for aging parents.

CHAPTER 5

Emotional Support for Caregivers

Recognizing and Managing Caregiver Stress

Generation X caregivers often face significant levels of stress as they navigate the responsibilities of caring for their aging parents. It is crucial for caregivers to recognize and manage this stress to maintain their own well-being. By acknowledging the signs of caregiver stress, such as fatigue, irritability, sleep disturbances, and feelings of overwhelm, caregivers can take proactive steps to address their emotional needs.

Managing caregiver stress involves implementing effective coping strategies. This may include engaging in stress-reducing activities such as exercise, meditation, deep breathing exercises, or engaging in hobbies and activities that bring joy and relaxation. Setting realistic expectations and boundaries, and learning to delegate tasks and ask for help, can also alleviate caregiver stress.

Self-Care Strategies for Generation X Caregivers

Self-care is essential for Generation X caregivers to maintain their physical, emotional, and mental well-being. Caregivers must prioritize their own needs and make time for activities that promote self-care. This may involve setting aside dedicated time for relaxation, engaging in activities that bring joy and fulfillment, and practicing self-compassion.

Taking care of one's physical health is also crucial. This includes getting regular exercise, eating a balanced diet, and getting enough sleep. Caregivers should also schedule regular check-ups with their healthcare providers to monitor their own health and address any concerns.

Additionally, caregivers should be mindful of their emotional well-being. This may involve seeking support from friends, family, or support groups, as well as considering professional counseling or therapy. Journaling, practicing mindfulness, and engaging in activities that promote emotional well-being can also be beneficial.

Finding Support Networks and Resources

Generation X caregivers should actively seek out support networks and resources to help them navigate the challenges of caregiving. Connecting with other caregivers who are going through similar experiences can provide a sense of understanding, validation, and support. Caregiver support groups, both in-person and online, can be valuable sources of emotional support and practical advice.

Caregivers should also explore community resources and organizations that offer assistance and services for caregivers. These resources may include respite care programs, home health services, and educational workshops. By accessing these resources, caregivers can alleviate some of the caregiving burden and gain valuable knowledge and skills.

Coping with Grief and Loss in the Caregiving Journey

The caregiving journey often involves experiencing grief and loss as caregivers witness the decline of their aging parents' health and independence. It is important for Generation X caregivers to acknowledge and cope with these emotions in a healthy and supportive manner.

Coping with grief and loss involves allowing oneself to grieve and process the emotions that arise. This may include expressing feelings through journaling, talking to a trusted friend or therapist, or participating in grief support groups. It is important for caregivers to give themselves permission to mourn and seek support during this challenging time.

In addition, caregivers should practice self-compassion and be patient with themselves as they navigate the grieving process. It is normal to experience a range of emotions, including sadness, anger, guilt, and even relief. By acknowledging and accepting these emotions, caregivers can begin to heal and find ways to honor their loved ones' memory.

Finding healthy ways to remember and honor their loved ones can also be a part of the grieving process. This may involve creating a memory box, writing letters, or participating in activities that were meaningful to their aging parents. Engaging in rituals or ceremonies that hold significance can provide a sense of closure and comfort.

Furthermore, caregivers should be aware that grief is a personal and ongoing process. It is not something that can be rushed or resolved quickly. It is important for caregivers to be patient with themselves and allow themselves the time and space to heal. Emotional support for caregivers is crucial for Generation X caregivers to maintain their well- being throughout the caregiving journey.

Recognizing and managing caregiver stress, implementing self-care strategies, finding support networks and resources, and coping with grief and loss are essential components of emotional support. By acknowledging and addressing caregiver stress, caregivers can take proactive steps to manage their emotional well-being. Implementing effective coping strategies, practicing self- care, and seeking support from friends, family, and support groups can alleviate stress and promote emotional well-being.

Finding support networks and resources, such as caregiver support groups and community organizations, can provide caregivers with valuable emotional support and practical assistance. Accessing these resources can alleviate some of the caregiving burden and provide caregivers with knowledge and skills to navigate the challenges they face.

Coping with grief and loss is an inevitable part of the caregiving journey. By allowing oneself to grieve, seeking support, and practicing self-compassion, caregivers can navigate the grieving process in a healthy and supportive manner. Finding ways to remember and honor their loved ones can provide a sense of closure and comfort.

In conclusion, emotional support is essential for Generation X caregivers to maintain their well- being throughout the caregiving journey. By recognizing and managing caregiver stress, implementing self-care strategies, finding support networks and resources, and coping with grief and loss, caregivers can navigate the challenges of caregiving with resilience and compassion. In the next chapter, we will explore the importance of financial planning and resources for caregivers to ensure their own financial stability and security.

FAQS - CHAPTER 5

Emotional Support for Caregivers

How can I recognize and manage caregiver stress?

Recognizing and managing caregiver stress is crucial for your well-being. Here are some strategies:

1. Be aware of the signs: Recognize the signs of caregiver stress, which may include fatigue, irritability, sleep disturbances, changes in appetite, or feelings of overwhelm and sadness.

2. Practice self-awareness: Pay attention to your own emotions and physical well-being. Take regular breaks and listen to your body's needs.

3. Seek support: Reach out to family, friends, or support groups to share your feelings and experiences. They can provide emotional support and understanding.

4. Set boundaries: Establish boundaries to protect your own well-being. Learn to say no when necessary and recognize your limitations.

5. Prioritize self-care: Make self-care a priority. Engage in activities that promote your physical, emotional, and mental well-being. This can include exercise, hobbies, relaxation techniques, or seeking therapy or counseling.

6. Utilize respite care: Take advantage of respite care services to provide temporary relief and time for yourself. This can help prevent burnout and allow you to recharge.

What are some self-care strategies that can help me as a Generation X caregiver?

Self-care is essential for maintaining your well-being as a Generation X caregiver. Here are some self-care strategies to consider:

1. Prioritize your own needs: Recognize that taking care of yourself is not selfish but necessary for your ability to provide care. Make time for activities that bring you joy and relaxation.

2. Establish a self-care routine: Incorporate self-care activities into your daily or weekly routine. This can include exercise, meditation, journaling, spending time with loved ones, pursuing hobbies, or engaging in creative outlets.

3. Practice stress management techniques: Find stress management techniques that work for you, such as deep breathing exercises, mindfulness meditation, or engaging in activities that help you relax and unwind.

4. Seek support: Reach out to support networks, such as caregiver support groups or online communities, where you can connect with others who understand your experiences and provide support and advice.

5. Delegate and ask for help: Don't hesitate to ask for help from family members, friends, or professional caregivers. Share the caregiving responsibilities to lighten your load.

6. Take breaks: Schedule regular breaks and respite care to give yourself time to rest and rejuvenate. Use this time to engage in activities that bring you joy and help you recharge.

Are there support networks and resources available for caregivers?

Yes, there are support networks and resources available for caregivers. Here are some options to consider:

1. Local caregiver support groups: Look for local caregiver support groups in your community. These groups provide a safe space to share experiences, receive emotional support, and exchange practical advice with other caregivers.

2. Online caregiver communities: Join online caregiver communities or forums where you can connect with caregivers from around the world. These platforms offer a space to share stories, ask questions, and find support.

3. Caregiver organizations and associations: Many organizations and associations focus on supporting caregivers. They provide resources, educational materials, and access to support networks. Examples include the Family Caregiver Alliance, National Alliance for Caregiving, and AARP.

4. Caregiver helplines and hotlines: Look for helplines or hotlines specifically dedicated to supporting caregivers. These services can provide guidance, emotional support, and referrals to local resources.

5. Respite care services: Explore respite care services in your area. These services offer temporary relief for caregivers by providing trained professionals who can step in and care for your loved one, allowing you to take a break.

6. Professional counseling or therapy: Consider seeking professional counseling or therapy to address the emotional challenges of caregiving. Therapists or counselors who specialize in caregiver support can provide guidance, coping strategies, and a safe space to process your emotions.

How can I cope with grief and loss throughout the caregiving journey?

Coping with grief and loss throughout the caregiving journey can be challenging. Here are some strategies to consider:

1. Allow yourself to grieve: Recognize that grief is a natural response to loss. Give yourself permission to experience and express your emotions, whether it's sadness, anger, or confusion.

2. Seek support: Reach out to friends, family, or support groups who can provide understanding and empathy during this difficult time. Consider joining a grief support group where you can connect with others who have experienced similar losses.

3. Take care of yourself: Prioritize self-care activities that promote your emotional well-being, such as engaging in hobbies, practicing mindfulness or meditation, or seeking therapy or counseling.

4. Honor your loved one's memory: Find ways to honor and remember your loved one. This can include creating a memory box, writing in a journal, or participating in

activities that were meaningful to them. Celebrate their life and the impact they had on you and others.

5. Seek professional help if needed: If you find that your grief is overwhelming or interfering with your daily life, consider seeking professional help from a therapist or counselor who specializes in grief and loss. They can provide guidance and support as you navigate through the grieving process.

6. Give yourself time and be patient: Grief is a personal journey, and it takes time to heal. Be patient with yourself and allow yourself to grieve at your own pace. Remember that everyone's grief journey is unique, and there is no right or wrong way to grieve.

Remember, it's important to prioritize your own emotional well-being and seek support when needed. Taking care of yourself during the grieving process is essential for your overall well-being as a caregiver.

CHAPTER 6

Promoting Independence and Well-being for Aging Parents

Creating a Safe and Comfortable Home Environment

Creating a safe and comfortable home environment is essential for promoting independence and well-being for aging parents. Generation X caregivers should assess their loved one's living space and make necessary modifications to ensure safety and accessibility.

This may involve installing grab bars in bathrooms, removing tripping hazards, improving lighting, and arranging furniture to accommodate mobility aids. Caregivers should also consider the layout of the home and make adjustments to facilitate ease of movement and navigation.

In addition to physical modifications, caregivers should also ensure that their loved one's home is equipped with necessary assistive devices, such as handrails, shower chairs, and emergency call systems. These devices can provide added security and peace of mind for both the aging parent and the caregiver.

Fostering Companionship and Social Engagement

Maintaining social connections and fostering companionship is vital for the well-being of aging parents. Generation X caregivers should encourage and facilitate opportunities for their loved ones to engage with others and participate in social activities.

This may involve arranging regular visits with friends and family members, encouraging participation in community events or senior centers, or exploring virtual social platforms for connecting with others. Caregivers should also consider enrolling their loved ones in classes or clubs that align with their interests, such as art, music, or exercise groups.

By promoting social engagement, caregivers can help combat feelings of loneliness and isolation that can often accompany aging. Regular social interactions can enhance cognitive function, emotional well-being, and overall quality of life for aging parents.

Supporting Emotional Well-being and Sense of Purpose

Supporting the emotional well-being and sense of purpose of aging parents is crucial for their overall well-being. Generation X caregivers should actively engage in conversations that promote self-reflection, encourage positive thinking, and validate their loved one's feelings and experiences.

Caregivers can help their aging parents maintain a sense of purpose by involving them in decision-making processes, seeking their input on family matters, and encouraging them to pursue activities that bring them joy and fulfillment. This may involve volunteering, mentoring, or engaging in hobbies or creative pursuits.

Additionally, caregivers should be attentive to their loved one's emotional needs and provide a supportive and empathetic presence. This may involve actively listening, offering reassurance, and seeking professional help if needed.

By prioritizing emotional well-being, caregivers can contribute to a positive and fulfilling aging experience for their aging parents.

Engaging in Meaningful Activities and Hobbies

Engaging in meaningful activities and hobbies is essential for promoting independence and well-being in aging parents. Generation X caregivers should encourage their loved ones to pursue activities that bring them joy, fulfillment, and a sense of purpose.

Caregivers can help identify activities and hobbies that align with their loved one's interests and abilities. This may involve exploring new hobbies or rekindling old passions. Engaging in activities such as gardening, painting, playing an instrument, or participating in book clubs can provide a sense of accomplishment and enjoyment.

In addition to individual pursuits, caregivers should also encourage their aging parents to engage in group activities and social events. This may include joining community organizations, participating in exercise classes, or attending cultural events. These activities not only provide opportunities for social interaction but also contribute to cognitive stimulation and overall well- being.

Furthermore, caregivers should consider the benefits of intergenerational activities and encourage their loved ones to spend time with younger family members or volunteer in settings where they can interact with younger generations. These interactions can foster a sense of purpose, provide opportunities for mentorship, and create meaningful connections.

By promoting engagement in meaningful activities and hobbies, caregivers can enhance their loved one's quality of life, promote cognitive function, and foster a sense of independence and well-being.

Fostering companionship and social engagement is equally important. Encouraging social activities, facilitating family gatherings, and exploring community programs can help combat feelings of loneliness and isolation. Embracing technology and considering pet companionship can also provide valuable sources of companionship and connection.

Additionally, supporting our parents' emotional well-being and helping them maintain a sense of purpose is crucial for their overall happiness and fulfillment. By fostering open communication, encouraging autonomy and decision-making, and supporting their interests and hobbies, we can empower them to lead meaningful lives. Promoting physical and mental stimulation, providing opportunities for contribution, and offering emotional support are additional strategies that can make a significant impact.

Encouraging our parents to engage in meaningful activities and hobbies is a powerful way to enhance their well-being and sense of purpose. By exploring their interests, providing necessary resources, and offering support and encouragement, we can help them find joy and fulfillment in their daily lives.

As Generation X caregivers, it is our responsibility to create nurturing environments that promote independence, dignity, and overall well-being for our aging parents. By implementing the strategies discussed in this chapter, we can make a profound difference in their lives. Let us continue to advocate for person-centered care and ensure that our parents thrive as they age gracefully at home.

In conclusion, promoting independence and well-being for our aging parents is a multifaceted endeavor that requires careful consideration of their physical, social, and emotional needs. By creating a safe and comfortable home environment, we can minimize the risk of accidents and enhance their overall safety. Installing safety features, ensuring proper lighting, and organizing belongings are just a few strategies that can make a significant difference.

FAQS - CHAPTER 6

Promoting Independence and Well-being for Aging Parents

How can I create a safe and comfortable home environment for my parents?

Creating a safe and comfortable home environment for your parents involves considering their physical and cognitive abilities. Here are some strategies:

1. Remove hazards: Conduct a thorough assessment of the home and remove any potential hazards such as loose rugs, cluttered walkways, or slippery surfaces.

2. Install safety features: Install grab bars in bathrooms, handrails on staircases, and adequate lighting throughout the house to enhance safety and accessibility.

3. Ensure proper lighting: Make sure all areas of the home are well-lit to prevent falls and improve visibility.

4. Arrange furniture for easy navigation: Rearrange furniture to create clear pathways and ensure that it is easy for your parents to move around without obstacles.

5. Consider assistive devices: If needed, provide assistive devices such as shower chairs, raised toilet seats, or mobility aids to support your parents' independence and safety.

6. Organize belongings: Help your parents organize their belongings in a way that is easily accessible and reduces the risk of falls or accidents.

7. Regular maintenance: Regularly check and maintain home systems such as heating, cooling, and plumbing to ensure a comfortable and safe living environment.

What are some strategies for fostering companionship and social engagement?

Fostering companionship and social engagement is important for your parents' well-being. Here are some strategies to consider:

1. Encourage social activities: Encourage your parents to participate in social activities such as joining clubs, attending community events, or volunteering. These activities provide opportunities for social interaction and engagement.

2. Facilitate family gatherings: Arrange regular family gatherings or outings to bring your parents together with loved ones. This can help foster a sense of belonging and connection.

3. Explore senior centers or community programs: Research local senior centers or community programs that offer social activities, classes, or support groups specifically designed for older adults. Encourage your parents to participate in these programs.

4. Utilize technology: Help your parents navigate technology to stay connected with family and friends. Teach them how to use video calling platforms or social media to maintain relationships and engage in virtual social interactions.

5. Consider pet companionship: If appropriate, consider getting a pet for your parents. Pets can provide companionship, reduce feelings of loneliness, and encourage physical activity.

6. Foster intergenerational connections: Encourage interactions between your parents and younger generations, such as grandchildren or local youth groups. This can create meaningful connections and opportunities for sharing experiences and knowledge.

How can I support my parents' emotional well-being and help them maintain a sense of purpose?

Supporting your parents' emotional well-being and helping them maintain a sense of purpose is essential for their overall well-being. Here are some strategies:

1. Foster open communication: Maintain open and honest communication with your parents, allowing them to express their feelings, concerns, and desires. Listen actively and validate their emotions.

2. Encourage autonomy and decision-making: Involve your parents in decision-making processes regarding their care, daily activities, and plans. This helps them maintain a sense of control and purpose.

3. Support their interests and hobbies: Encourage your parents to pursue activities and hobbies they enjoy. This can provide a sense of fulfillment and purpose in their daily lives.

4. Promote physical and mental stimulation: Engage your parents in activities that promote physical and mental stimulation, such as puzzles, reading, exercise, or learning new skills. This helps maintain cognitive function and a sense of accomplishment.

5. Provide opportunities for contribution: Help your parents find ways to contribute to their community or family, such as volunteering, mentoring, or sharing their knowledge and skills with others. This can give them a sense of purpose and fulfillment.

6. Offer emotional support: Be there for your parents emotionally, providing a listening ear, empathy, and reassurance. Offer support during challenging times and encourage them to seek professional help if needed.

What are some ways to encourage my parents to engage in meaningful activities and hobbies?

Encouraging your parents to engage in meaningful activities and hobbies can enhance their well-being and sense of purpose. Here are some strategies:

1. Explore their interests: Talk to your parents about their interests and passions. Encourage them to pursue activities or hobbies that align with their interests, whether it's painting, gardening, playing an instrument, or joining a book club.

2. Provide resources and materials: Ensure that your parents have access to the necessary resources and materials for their chosen activities or hobbies. This may involve providing art supplies, gardening tools, or books.

3. Offer support and encouragement: Be supportive and encouraging as your parents explore new activities or hobbies. Help when needed and celebrate their achievements and progress.

4. Create a dedicated space: Set up a dedicated space in their home where they can engage in their chosen activities or hobbies comfortably.

5. Help them explore new hobbies or interests that align with their abilities and interests.

6. Provide necessary resources or equipment for their chosen activities.

7. Encourage participation in community classes or workshops related to their interests.

8. Arrange regular outings to cultural events, museums, or parks.
9. Offer to participate in activities together, fostering bonding and shared experiences.

CHAPTER 7

Flexibility in Caregiving

Managing Time and Multiple Responsibilities

Generation X caregivers often find themselves juggling multiple responsibilities, including caregiving, work, and personal commitments. Managing time effectively is crucial to maintain balance and prevent burnout.

Caregivers should prioritize tasks and create a schedule that allows for flexibility and breaks. This may involve delegating certain responsibilities to other family members or hiring professional caregivers to provide support. By effectively managing time, caregivers can ensure that they have the energy and resources to meet the needs of their aging parents while also taking care of themselves.

Flexible Scheduling Options for Caregivers

Flexibility in scheduling is essential for Generation X caregivers who often have demanding work schedules and other commitments. Employers should be encouraged to provide flexible work arrangements, such as telecommuting, flexible hours, or job-sharing options. This allows caregivers to balance their caregiving responsibilities with their professional obligations.

In addition, caregivers should explore alternative care options, such as adult day programs or respite care services, that offer flexible scheduling.

These services can provide temporary relief for caregivers, allowing them to attend to personal needs or take breaks while ensuring their loved ones receive the care they need.

Tailoring Care Plans to Meet Specific Needs and Preferences

Each aging parent has unique needs and preferences, and it is essential for Generation X caregivers to tailor care plans accordingly. This involves actively listening to their loved ones, involving them in decision-making processes, and respecting their autonomy.

Caregivers should consider their loved one's preferences for daily routines, activities, and personal care. By incorporating these preferences into the care plan, caregivers can promote a sense of independence and dignity for their aging parents.

Furthermore, caregivers should regularly reassess and adjust care plans as their loved one's needs change over time. This flexibility ensures that the care provided remains relevant and effective in meeting their evolving requirements.

Respite Care and Taking Breaks for Caregivers

Taking breaks and seeking respite care is crucial for the wellbeing of Generation X caregivers. Caregiving can be physically and emotionally demanding, and caregivers need time to recharge and take care of their own needs.

Respite care services provide temporary relief for caregivers by offering professional care for their loved ones.

This allows caregivers to take breaks, attend to personal matters, or simply rest and rejuvenate. It is important for caregivers to recognize the importance of respite care and not hesitate to seek support when needed.

Caregivers should actively plan and schedule regular breaks for themselves. This may involve coordinating with family members or friends to provide temporary care for their aging parents. By taking breaks, caregivers can prevent burnout, reduce stress, and maintain their own physical and mental well-being.

During these breaks, caregivers should engage in activities that promote self-care and relaxation. This may include pursuing hobbies, exercising, spending time with loved ones, or simply taking time for themselves. By prioritizing their own needs and well-being, caregivers can continue to provide quality care for their aging parents.

In addition to respite care, caregivers should also seek emotional support from friends, family, or support groups. Sharing experiences, concerns, and emotions with others who understand the challenges of caregiving can provide a sense of validation and relief. Caregivers should not hesitate to reach out for support when needed.

Flexibility in caregiving is essential for Generation X caregivers to effectively manage their responsibilities and maintain their own well-being. By managing time, exploring flexible scheduling options, tailoring care plans to meet specific needs and preferences, and taking breaks through respite care, caregivers can navigate the caregiving journey with resilience and compassion.

Additionally, flexibility in caregiving is crucial for Generation X caregivers to effectively manage their responsibilities and maintain their own well-being. By prioritizing tasks, creating a flexible schedule, and seeking support from family members or professional caregivers, caregivers can balance their caregiving duties with work and personal commitments.

Employers should be encouraged to provide flexible work arrangements, allowing caregivers to fulfill their professional obligations while attending to the needs of their aging parents. Exploring alternative care options, such as adult day programs or respite care services, can also provide temporary relief for caregivers, ensuring their loved ones receive the care they need while caregivers take breaks or attend to personal needs.

Tailoring care plans to meet the specific needs and preferences of aging parents is essential. By actively listening, involving them in decision-making, and respecting their autonomy, caregivers can promote a sense of independence and dignity. Regularly reassessing and adjusting care plans as needs change over time ensures that the care provided remains relevant and effective.

Taking breaks and seeking respite care is crucial for caregivers' well-being. Caregiving can be physically and emotionally demanding, and caregivers need time to recharge and take care of their own needs. By actively planning and scheduling regular breaks, caregivers can prevent burnout and maintain their own physical and mental well-being. Engaging in self-care activities and seeking emotional support from others who understand the challenges of caregiving are also important aspects of maintaining caregiver well-being.

In conclusion, flexibility in caregiving allows Generation X caregivers to navigate their responsibilities with resilience and compassion. By managing time effectively, exploring flexible scheduling options, tailoring care plans, and taking breaks through respite care, caregivers can provide quality care for their aging parents while also taking care of themselves. Let us continue to advocate for flexible caregiving options and support systems that empower caregivers to thrive in their caregiving journey.

FAQS – CHAPTER 7

Flexibility in Caregiving

How can I effectively manage my time and multiple responsibilities as a caregiver?

1. Prioritize tasks and create a schedule or to-do list to stay organized.
2. Delegate tasks to other family members or hire professional caregivers for certain responsibilities.
3. Utilize technology, such as calendar apps or reminder systems, to help manage appointments and medication schedules.
4. Seek support from support groups or online communities to share experiences and learn time management strategies.
5. Take care of your own physical and mental health to ensure you have the energy and focus to manage multiple responsibilities.

Are there flexible scheduling options available for caregivers?

1. Explore part-time or flexible work options that allow you to balance caregiving responsibilities.
2. Discuss flexible scheduling arrangements with your employer, such as working remotely or adjusting your hours.

3. Look into respite care services that provide temporary relief for caregivers, allowing for more flexibility in scheduling.

How can I tailor care plans to meet my parents' specific needs and preferences?

1. Involve your parents in the care planning process to understand their preferences and goals.
2. Consult with healthcare professionals to assess your parents' specific needs and develop a personalized care plan.
3. Regularly reassess and adjust the care plan as your parents' needs change over time.
4. Consider cultural, religious, or personal beliefs when tailoring care plans to ensure they align with your parents' values.

What options are available for respite care and taking breaks as a caregiver?

1. Seek assistance from family members or close friends who can provide temporary relief and take over caregiving duties.
2. Explore respite care services that offer short-term care in a facility or at home, allowing you to take breaks.
3. Look into adult day care centers where your parents can spend time socializing and engaging in activities while you take a break.

4. Consider hiring professional caregivers for temporary periods to provide respite care.

5. Utilize community resources or support groups that may offer volunteer assistance or respite care programs.

Note: These answers are based on general knowledge and may not be applicable to every individual situation. It is important to consider the specific needs and preferences of your parents when implementing these strategies. Additionally, local resources and regulations may vary, so it is advisable to research and consult with professionals in your area.

CHAPTER 8

Navigating Healthcare Systems and Resources

Understanding Medicare, Medicaid, and Insurance Coverage

Understanding the complexities of healthcare systems and insurance coverage is crucial for Generation X caregivers as they navigate the healthcare needs of their aging parents.

Caregivers should familiarize themselves with Medicare and Medicaid, as well as private insurance options, to ensure their loved ones have access to necessary healthcare services.

By understanding the eligibility criteria, coverage options, and limitations of these programs, caregivers can make informed decisions regarding their loved one's healthcare. It is important to stay updated on any changes or updates to these programs to ensure that their aging parents receive the appropriate care and support.

Accessing Community Resources and Support Services

Community resources and support services play a vital role in meeting the healthcare needs of aging parents. Generation X caregivers should actively seek out and utilize these resources to enhance the well-being of their loved ones.

Community resources may include senior centers, adult day programs, meal delivery services, and transportation services. These resources can provide social engagement, nutritional support, and assistance with daily activities. Caregivers should research and connect with local organizations that offer these services to ensure their loved ones have access to the support they need.

Additionally, support services such as caregiver support groups, counseling services, and respite care programs can provide valuable assistance and emotional support for caregivers themselves. By accessing these resources, caregivers can alleviate some of the burdens of caregiving and find guidance and understanding from others who are going through similar experiences.

Managing Medications and Medical Appointments

Managing medications and medical appointments is a critical aspect of caregiving for aging parents. Generation X caregivers should establish effective systems to ensure that their loved ones receive the appropriate medications and attend necessary medical appointments.

This may involve creating medication management systems, such as pill organizers or medication reminder apps, to help caregivers and their aging parents stay organized and on track with medication schedules. Caregivers should also maintain open communication with healthcare providers to ensure a clear understanding of medication instructions and potential side effects.

Scheduling and coordinating medical appointments can be challenging, especially when multiple specialists are involved. Caregivers should maintain a comprehensive calendar and utilize reminder systems to keep track of appointments.

They should also accompany their aging parents to medical visits to provide support, ask questions, and ensure that all concerns are addressed.

Legal and Financial Considerations for Aging Parents

Legal and financial considerations are important aspects of caregiving for aging parents. Generation X caregivers should proactively address these considerations to ensure the well- being and protection of their loved ones.

Legal considerations may include establishing power of attorney, creating advance directives, and updating wills or trusts. Caregivers should consult with legal professionals to navigate these processes and ensure that their aging parents' wishes are documented and legally protected.

Financial considerations involve managing finances, accessing benefits, and planning for long- term care. Caregivers should work closely with financial advisors or elder law attorneys to understand available resources, such as pensions, Social Security benefits, and long-term care insurance. They should also explore options for managing and protecting assets, such as setting up trusts or exploring Medicaid planning.

By addressing legal and financial considerations, caregivers can provide a secure and stable future for their aging parents, ensuring that their healthcare needs are met, and their assets are protected.

Non-Emergency Medical Transportation (NEMT) Services

The Importance of Reliable Transportation for Medical Appointments

As a Generation X caregiver, I firmly believe that person-centered homecare cannot be achieved without the inclusion of Non-Emergency Medical Transportation (NEMT) services. Navigating healthcare systems and resources is already a complex task, and reliable transportation is a crucial component in ensuring that aging parents can access necessary medical appointments and healthcare services.

Transportation barriers can significantly hinder the ability of aging parents to receive timely medical care, potentially leading to health complications. Moreover, limited transportation options can restrict their engagement in social activities and access to community resources. Recognizing these challenges, caregivers must seek solutions to ensure their loved ones can attend medical appointments and maintain their overall health.

NEMT services offer a valuable solution for caregivers seeking reliable transportation options for their aging parents. These services provide transportation to and from medical appointments, ensuring that aging parents can access the care they need. By researching and connecting with NEMT providers in their area, caregivers can understand the services offered and the eligibility criteria. NEMT services often cater to individuals with specific medical needs, such as wheelchair accessibility or specialized medical equipment, ensuring a safe and comfortable journey for aging parents.

Utilizing NEMT services brings numerous benefits to the healthcare needs of aging parents. Firstly, it provides a convenient and reliable transportation option, eliminating the stress and logistical challenges of arranging transportation for every medical appointment. NEMT services employ trained drivers who are knowledgeable about the specific needs of aging individuals, ensuring a comfortable and safe journey, especially for those with mobility limitations or medical equipment requirements.

Additionally, NEMT services help reduce the risk of missed or delayed medical appointments. Timely access to healthcare is crucial for managing chronic conditions, receiving necessary treatments, and preventing potential health complications. By utilizing NEMT services, caregivers can ensure that their aging parents receive the care they need in a timely manner.

Furthermore, NEMT services provide peace of mind for caregivers, knowing that their loved ones are in capable hands during transportation. This allows caregivers to focus on other aspects of caregiving and alleviates the burden of arranging transportation for every medical appointment.

Reliable transportation is crucial for ensuring that aging parents can access necessary medical appointments and healthcare services. Generation X caregivers should recognize the importance of reliable transportation and its impact on their loved ones' wellbeing.

Transportation barriers can prevent aging parents from receiving timely medical care, leading to potential health complications. Lack of transportation options may also limit their ability to engage in social activities or access community resources.

It is essential for caregivers to address these challenges and seek solutions to ensure their loved ones can attend medical appointments and maintain their overall health.

In conclusion, as a Generation X caregiver, I firmly believe that person-centered homecare cannot be achieved without the inclusion of NEMT services. Reliable transportation is essential for accessing medical appointments, and NEMT services offer convenience, safety, and peace of mind for caregivers. By utilizing NEMT services, caregivers can ensure that their aging parents have the means to access the care they need in a timely.

Accessing NEMT Services for Aging Parents

Non-Emergency Medical Transportation (NEMT) services offer a valuable solution for caregivers seeking reliable transportation options for their aging parents. NEMT services provide transportation to and from medical appointments, ensuring that aging parents can access the care they need.

Caregivers should research and connect with NEMT providers in their area to understand the services offered and the eligibility criteria. NEMT services often cater to individuals with specific medical needs, such as wheelchair accessibility or specialized medical equipment. By utilizing NEMT services, caregivers can ensure that their aging parents have safe and reliable transportation to medical appointments.

Benefits of Utilizing NEMT for Healthcare Needs

Utilizing NEMT services offers several benefits for the healthcare needs of aging parents. Firstly, it provides a convenient and reliable transportation option, eliminating the stress and logistical challenges of arranging transportation for medical appointments.

NEMT services are often equipped with trained drivers who are knowledgeable about the specific needs of aging individuals, ensuring a comfortable and safe journey. This can be particularly important for those with mobility limitations or medical equipment requirements.

Additionally, NEMT services can help reduce the risk of missed or delayed medical appointments. Timely access to healthcare is crucial for managing chronic conditions, receiving necessary treatments, and preventing potential health complications. By utilizing NEMT services, caregivers can ensure that their aging parents receive the care they need in a timely manner.

Furthermore, NEMT services can provide peace of mind for caregivers, knowing that their loved ones are in capable hands during transportation. This allows caregivers to focus on other aspects of caregiving and alleviates the burden of arranging transportation for every medical appointment.

Navigating healthcare systems and resources is a complex task for Generation X caregivers. By understanding Medicare, Medicaid, and insurance coverage, caregivers can ensure their aging parents have access to necessary healthcare services. Accessing community resources and support services can enhance the well-being of aging parents and provide valuable assistance and emotional support for caregivers themselves.

Managing medications and medical appointments is critical, and caregivers should establish effective systems to ensure their loved ones receive the appropriate medications and attend necessary appointments. Legal and financial considerations should also be addressed to protect the well-being and assets of aging parents.

Reliable transportation is essential for accessing medical appointments, and caregivers should recognize the importance of reliable transportation and explore options such as Non- Emergency Medical Transportation (NEMT) services. Utilizing NEMT services offers convenience, safety, and peace of mind for caregivers and ensures that aging parents can access the care they need in a timely manner.

In conclusion, by navigating healthcare systems and utilizing available resources, Generation X caregivers can ensure that their aging parents receive the necessary care and support. Let us continue to advocate for accessible and comprehensive healthcare services and support systems that empower caregivers to navigate the healthcare journey with confidence and compassion.

FAQS – CHAPTER 8

Navigating Healthcare Systems and Resources

Can you help me understand Medicare, Medicaid, and insurance coverage for my parents?

1. Medicare is a federal health insurance program for individuals aged 65 and older or those with certain disabilities. It covers hospital stays, doctor visits, prescription drugs, and more.

2. Medicaid is a joint federal and state program that provides health coverage for low-income individuals, including some seniors. Eligibility and coverage vary by state.

3. Private insurance plans, such as employer-sponsored plans or individual plans, may provide additional coverage options for your parents. It is important to review the specific terms and benefits of their insurance plans.

What community resources and support services are available for aging parents?

1. Area Agencies on Aging (AAA) provide information and assistance on local resources, including home care services, meal programs, transportation, and more.

2. Senior centers offer various programs and activities for social engagement, health promotion, and support.

3. Non-profit organizations, such as the Alzheimer's Association or American Cancer Society, provide resources and support for specific health conditions.
4. Local community and faith-based organizations may offer volunteer services, respite care, or support groups.

How can I effectively manage medications and medical appointments for my parents?

1. Create a medication management system, such as pill organizers or medication reminder apps, to ensure medications are taken correctly and on time.
2. Maintain an up-to-date list of medications, including dosages and instructions, and share it with healthcare providers.
3. Use a calendar or scheduling system to keep track of medical appointments, tests, and follow-ups.
4. Consider utilizing pharmacy services, such as medication synchronization or home delivery, to simplify medication management.

What legal and financial considerations should I be aware of for my parents' care?

1. Consult with an elder law attorney to discuss legal documents like power of attorney, living wills, and healthcare proxies.
2. Review and update your parents' financial and estate plans, including wills, trusts, and beneficiary designations.

3. Explore long-term care insurance options and understand the coverage and benefits they provide.

4. Research government programs, such as Veterans Affairs benefits or Social Security, that may offer financial assistance for seniors.

Can you provide information on non-emergency medical transportation (NEMT) services and their benefits for healthcare needs?

1. Non-emergency medical transportation (NEMT) services provide transportation to medical appointments for individuals who have difficulty accessing transportation on their own.

2. NEMT services are typically covered by Medicaid and some private insurance plans for eligible individuals.

3. These services can be beneficial for seniors who may have mobility limitations or require assistance during transportation.

4. NEMT services often provide door-to-door transportation, ensuring safe and reliable transportation to medical appointments, therapies, and other healthcare-related destinations.

5. Some NEMT providers offer specialized vehicles equipped with wheelchair ramps or lifts to accommodate individuals with mobility devices.

6. NEMT services can help ensure that seniors receive timely and necessary medical care, reducing the risk of missed appointments or delays in treatment.

Note: NEMT services may vary by location and insurance coverage. It is advisable to check with your parents' insurance provider or local healthcare agencies to understand the specific NEMT options available to them.

CHAPTER 9

End-of-Life Planning and Palliative Care

Discussing End-of-Life Wishes with Aging Parents

Discussing end-of-life wishes with aging parents is a difficult but essential conversation for Generation X caregivers. It is important to have open and honest discussions about their loved ones' preferences for medical care, life-sustaining treatments, and final arrangements.

Caregivers should approach these conversations with sensitivity and empathy, creating a safe space for their aging parents to express their wishes and concerns. It is crucial to actively listen and validate their feelings, ensuring that their autonomy and dignity are respected.

By having these discussions early on, caregivers can ensure that their loved ones' wishes are documented and can be honored when the time comes. This can provide peace of mind for both the aging parents and the caregivers, knowing that their wishes will be respected and followed.

Exploring Palliative Care and Hospice Options

Palliative care and hospice services play a vital role in providing comfort and support to aging parents in the final stages of life. Generation X caregivers should explore these options to ensure that their loved ones receive the appropriate care and support during this challenging time.

Palliative care focuses on providing relief from pain and symptoms, improving quality of life, and addressing the emotional, social, and spiritual needs of individuals with serious illnesses. Hospice care, on the other hand, is specifically designed for individuals with a terminal illness and focuses on providing comfort and support in the final stages of life.

Caregivers should research and connect with palliative care and hospice providers to understand the services offered and the eligibility criteria. These services can provide specialized medical care, emotional support, and assistance with end-of-life planning. By exploring these options, caregivers can ensure that their aging parents receive the appropriate care and support tailored to their specific needs.

Providing Comfort and Support in the Final Stages of Life

Providing comfort and support to aging parents in the final stages of life is a profound responsibility for Generation X caregivers. It is important to create a peaceful and supportive environment that promotes dignity, comfort, and emotional wellbeing.

Caregivers should work closely with healthcare professionals to manage pain and symptoms effectively, ensuring that their loved ones are as comfortable as possible. This may involve medication management, physical therapy, or alternative therapies such as music or art therapy.

Emotional support is equally important during this time. Caregivers should provide a compassionate presence, actively listen, and validate their loved ones' emotions and concerns. Engaging in meaningful conversations, reminiscing, and creating opportunities for connection and closure can provide comfort and support during this challenging time.

Additionally, caregivers should ensure that their loved ones' spiritual and cultural needs are respected and addressed. This may involve arranging visits from spiritual leaders, facilitating religious or cultural practices, or providing access to resources that align with their beliefs and values.

Grief and Bereavement Support for Caregivers

Grief and bereavement support is crucial for Generation X caregivers as they navigate the loss of their aging parents. Caregivers should recognize that their own emotional well-being is equally important and seek support to process their grief and navigate the bereavement journey.

Support groups, counseling services, and online resources can provide valuable assistance for caregivers experiencing grief and loss. Connecting with others who have gone through similar experiences can offer comfort, validation, and guidance during this challenging time.

Self-care is also essential for caregivers during the grieving process. Engaging in activities that promote self-care, such as exercise, journaling, or seeking moments of solitude, can help caregivers process their emotions and find moments of peace and healing.

By prioritizing their own well-being and seeking support, caregivers can navigate the grief and bereavement journey with resilience and find ways to honor the memory of their loved ones.

End-of-life planning and palliative care are crucial aspects of caregiving for aging parents. Generation X caregivers should engage in open and honest discussions about end-of- life wishes, explore palliative care and hospice options, provide comfort and support in the final stages of life, and seek grief and bereavement support for themselves. By addressing these aspects, caregivers can ensure that their loved ones receive compassionate care and support throughout the end-of-life journey.

By discussing end-of-life wishes with aging parents, exploring palliative care and hospice options, and providing comfort and support in the final stages of life, caregivers can ensure that their loved ones receive the appropriate care and support tailored to their specific needs.

Caregivers should approach these conversations with sensitivity and empathy, creating a safe space for their aging parents to express their wishes and concerns. By having these discussions early on, caregivers can ensure that their loved ones' wishes are documented and can be honored when the time comes.

Palliative care and hospice services provide specialized medical care, emotional support, and assistance with end-of-life planning. Caregivers should research and connect with providers to understand the services offered and the eligibility criteria, ensuring that their aging parents receive the appropriate care and support during this challenging time.

Providing comfort and support in the final stages of life involves managing pain and symptoms effectively, providing emotional support, and addressing spiritual and cultural needs. By creating a peaceful and supportive environment that promotes dignity, comfort, and emotional well-being, caregivers can help their loved ones navigate this difficult time with grace and peace.

Grief and bereavement support is crucial for caregivers as they navigate the loss of their aging parents. By seeking support, engaging in self-care activities, and connecting with others who have gone through similar experiences, caregivers can process their grief and find moments of healing and peace.

In conclusion, end-of-life planning and palliative care require compassion, empathy, and support. Let us continue to advocate for accessible and comprehensive end-of-life care options and support systems that empower caregivers to navigate this journey with love, dignity, and grace.

FAQS – CHAPTER 9

End-of-Life Planning and Palliative Care

How can I initiate discussions about end-of-life wishes with my aging parents?

1. Choose an appropriate time and place for the conversation, ensuring privacy and minimal distractions.
2. Approach the topic with sensitivity and empathy, expressing your concern for their well-being and desire to honor their wishes.
3. Use open-ended questions to encourage dialogue and active listening, allowing your parents to express their thoughts and concerns.
4. Share your own thoughts and feelings about end-of-life planning to create a safe and open environment for discussion.
5. Consider involving a healthcare professional, such as a doctor or social worker, who can provide guidance and facilitate conversation.

What are the options for palliative care and hospice services?

1. Palliative care focuses on providing relief from symptoms and improving the quality of life for individuals with serious illnesses, regardless of their life expectancy.

2. Hospice care is a type of palliative care specifically designed for individuals with a life expectancy of six months or less.

3. Palliative care can be provided alongside curative treatments, while hospice care is typically provided when curative treatments are no longer effective or desired.

4. Both palliative care and hospice services can be provided at home, in hospitals, or in specialized facilities, depending on the individual's needs and preferences.

How can I provide comfort and support to my parents in the final stages of life?

1. Ensure open and honest communication, allowing your parents to express their fears, concerns, and wishes.

2. Provide physical comfort by ensuring pain management, maintaining personal hygiene, and assisting with daily activities.

3. Create a peaceful and comforting environment, incorporating familiar objects, music, or scents that bring comfort to your parents.

4. Offer emotional support by actively listening, validating their feelings, and providing reassurance and comfort.

5. Respect their autonomy and involve them in decision-making processes regarding their care and end-of-life wishes.

Are there grief and bereavement support services available for caregivers?

1. Many hospitals, hospice organizations, and community centers offer grief support groups or counseling services for caregivers.
2. Online resources and forums provide a platform for connecting with others who have experienced similar losses.
3. Seek support from friends, family, or religious/spiritual communities who can provide emotional support during the grieving process.
4. Consider reaching out to professional grief counselors or therapists who specialize in bereavement support.

CHAPTER 10

Technology and Innovations in Caregiving

Assistive Technologies for Aging Parents

Assistive technologies have revolutionized the way caregivers provide care for their aging parents. Generation X caregivers should explore the wide range of assistive technologies available to enhance the safety, independence, and well-being of their loved ones.

Assistive technologies can include devices such as smart home systems, wearable devices, and medical alert systems. These technologies can help monitor vital signs, detect falls, remind individuals to take medications, and help with daily activities. By incorporating assistive technologies into the caregiving routine, caregivers can enhance the quality of care provided while promoting a sense of independence for their aging parents.

Telehealth and Remote Monitoring

Telehealth and remote monitoring have become increasingly important in the caregiving landscape, especially considering the COVID-19 pandemic. Generation X caregivers should embrace these technologies to ensure that their aging parents have access to healthcare services from the comfort of their own homes.

Telehealth allows for virtual medical consultations, enabling aging parents to connect with healthcare professionals remotely. This can be particularly beneficial for individuals with mobility limitations or those living in rural areas with limited access to healthcare facilities. Remote monitoring technologies, such as wearable devices or home monitoring systems, can also provide real-time health data to healthcare providers, allowing for proactive and personalized care.

By utilizing telehealth and remote monitoring, caregivers can ensure that their aging parents receive timely medical care, reduce the need for unnecessary hospital visits, and promote overall health and well-being.

Mobile Apps and Digital Tools for Caregivers

Mobile apps and digital tools have transformed the way caregivers manage their responsibilities and access resources. Generation X caregivers should explore the wide range of mobile apps and digital tools available to support their caregiving journey.

Caregiver-specific apps can help with medication management, appointment scheduling, and tracking health information. These apps can provide reminders, organize medical records, and facilitate communication with healthcare providers. Digital tools, such as online support groups, educational resources, and caregiving forums, can also provide valuable information and emotional support for caregivers.

By incorporating mobile apps and digital tools into their caregiving routine, caregivers can streamline tasks, access information and resources, and find support from a community of fellow caregivers.

Ethical Considerations and Privacy in Technology Use

While technology offers numerous benefits for caregivers and their aging parents, it is important to consider ethical considerations and privacy concerns. Generation X caregivers should approach the use of technology in caregiving with careful consideration and respect for privacy.

Caregivers should ensure that the technologies they choose are secure and protect the privacy of their aging parents. This may involve researching and selecting reputable companies and products that prioritize data security and encryption. It is important to read and understand the privacy policies and terms of use associated with any technology being utilized.

Additionally, caregivers should have open and transparent conversations with their aging parents about the use of technology and obtain their informed consent. Respecting their loved ones' autonomy and privacy is paramount, and caregivers should involve them in the decision- making process regarding the use of specific technologies.

Ethical considerations also extend to the responsible and appropriate use of technology. Caregivers should use technology as a tool to enhance care and support, rather than relying solely on it.

It is important to maintain human connections and provide hands-on care, while utilizing technology as a supplement to improve efficiency and safety.

Furthermore, caregivers should regularly reassess the effectiveness and impact of the technologies being used. If a technology is not meeting the needs or preferences of their aging parents, caregivers should be open to exploring alternative options or discontinuing its use.

By approaching the use of technology in caregiving with ethical considerations and privacy in mind, Generation X caregivers can harness the benefits of technology while ensuring the dignity and well-being of their aging parents.

Assistive technologies offer a wide range of devices that can monitor vital signs, detect falls, and help with daily activities. Telehealth and remote monitoring enable aging parents to access healthcare services from home, reducing the need for unnecessary hospital visits. Mobile apps and digital tools streamline caregiving tasks and provide access to information and support.

However, it is important for caregivers to approach the use of technology with ethical considerations and respect for privacy. Caregivers should ensure that the technologies they choose prioritize data security and encryption, involve their aging parents in decision-making, and use technology as a supplement to human connections and hands-on care.

By harnessing the benefits of technology while considering ethical considerations and privacy concerns, Generation X caregivers can provide enhanced care and support for their aging parents.

Let us continue to embrace and advocate for the responsible and ethical use of technology in caregiving, ensuring the dignity and well-being of our loved ones.

In conclusion, technology and innovations in caregiving have transformed the way Generation X caregivers provide care for their aging parents. By exploring assistive technologies, embracing telehealth and remote monitoring, utilizing mobile apps and digital tools, and considering ethical considerations and privacy concerns, caregivers can enhance the safety, independence, and well-being of their loved ones.

FAQS - CHAPTER 10

Technology and Innovations in Caregiving

What assistive technologies are available to support aging parents?

1. Personal emergency response systems (PERS) allow seniors to call for help in case of emergencies.
2. Smart home devices, such as voice-activated assistants or automated lighting systems, can enhance safety and convenience.
3. Medication management systems, including pill dispensers with alarms or smartphone apps, help ensure medication adherence.
4. Fall detection devices or wearable sensors can alert caregivers or emergency services in the event of a fall.
5. GPS tracking devices or location-based apps can help locate seniors who may wander or get lost.

Can you provide information on telehealth and remote monitoring options?

1. Telehealth allows remote access to healthcare services, including virtual doctor visits, consultations, and monitoring.

2. Remote monitoring devices, such as blood pressure monitors or glucose meters, enable healthcare providers to track vital signs and health data remotely.

3. Video conferencing platforms facilitate communication between caregivers, seniors, and healthcare professionals for remote consultations and check-ins.

Are there any mobile apps or digital tools that can assist caregivers?

1. Caregiver apps, such as https://www.alto.com/ or https://www.caringbridge.org/, help organize and manage caregiving tasks, appointments, and medication schedules.
2. Health tracking apps, like MyFitnessPal or Medisafe, allow caregivers to monitor and track their parents' health data and medication adherence.
3. Memory aids and cognitive stimulation apps, such as Lumosity or MindMate, can support cognitive health and memory retention.
4. Communication apps, like Skype or FaceTime, enable video calls and virtual connections with distant family members or healthcare providers.

What ethical considerations and privacy concerns should I be aware of when using technology in caregiving?

1. Respect your parents' privacy and obtain their consent before implementing any technology solutions.
2. Ensure that any personal health information or data collected through technology is stored securely and in compliance with privacy regulations.

3. Be mindful of the potential for technology to replace human interaction and maintain a balance between technology use and personal caregiving.
4. Regularly review and update privacy settings on devices and apps to protect sensitive information.
5. Consider the limitations and potential risks of technology, such as technical failures or the need for human intervention in certain situations.

Note: Technology and innovations in caregiving are constantly evolving. It is important to stay informed about the latest advancements and consult with healthcare professionals or technology experts to determine the most suitable solutions for your specific caregiving needs. Additionally, it is crucial to consider the individual preferences and abilities of your aging parents when implementing technology in their care.

CHAPTER 11

Conclusion

Summary of Key Takeaways and Action Steps

Throughout this caregiving guide, we have explored the unique challenges and responsibilities faced by Generation X caregivers as they navigate the complex landscape of caring for their aging parents. Here is a summary of the key takeaways and action steps to guide you on your caregiving journey:

1. Understanding the Needs of Aging Parents: Take the time to understand your aging parents' physical, emotional, and social needs. This will help you provide personalized care and support.

2. Self-Care is Essential: Prioritize your own well-being and seek support from others. Remember that taking care of yourself allows you to better care for your loved ones.

3. Effective Communication: Maintain open and honest communication with your aging parents, healthcare providers, and other family members. This will ensure that everyone is on the same page and can work together to meet your loved ones' needs.

4. Navigating Healthcare Systems: Familiarize yourself with Medicare, Medicaid, and private insurance options to ensure your loved ones have access to necessary healthcare services. Stay updated on any changes or updates to these programs.

5. Accessing Community Resources: Utilize community resources and support services to enhance the well-being of your loved ones. Research and connect with local organizations that offer services such as senior centers, adult day programs, and transportation services.

6. Managing Medications and Medical Appointments: Establish effective systems to ensure your loved ones receive the appropriate medications and attend necessary medical appointments. Maintain open communication with healthcare providers and accompany your aging parents to medical visits.

7. Legal and Financial Considerations: Address legal and financial considerations, such as power of attorney, advance directives, and long-term care planning. Consult with legal and financial professionals to ensure your loved ones' wishes are documented and their assets are protected.

8. End-of-Life Planning and Palliative Care: Have open discussions about end-of-life wishes with your aging parents and explore palliative care and hospice options. Provide comfort and support in the final stages of life and seek grief and bereavement support for yourself.

9. Technology and Innovations in Caregiving: Explore assistive technologies, telehealth, and mobile apps to enhance care and support. Consider ethical considerations and privacy concerns when utilizing technology.

Final Words of Encouragement and Support

As a Generation X caregiver, you have taken on a significant role in caring for your aging parents. It is a journey filled with challenges, but also with moments of love, growth, and connection. Remember that you are not alone on this journey. Reach out for support from friends, family, support groups, and professional resources. Seek guidance from healthcare professionals, legal advisors, and financial experts to navigate the complexities of caregiving.

Take time to care for yourself, both physically and emotionally. Prioritize self-care activities that bring you joy and rejuvenation. Remember that you are not selfish about taking care of your own needs – it is essential for your well-being and your ability to provide the best care for your loved ones.

Embrace the power of communication and open dialogue. Engage in meaningful conversations with your aging parents, actively listen to their needs and wishes, and involve them in decision- making processes. Collaboration and understanding will strengthen your relationship and ensure that their care aligns with their values and preferences.

Embrace the advancements in technology and innovative solutions that can support your caregiving journey. Explore the vast array of resources available, from assistive technologies to telehealth services and mobile apps. However, always prioritize privacy and ethical considerations when utilizing these tools.

Remember that caregiving is a journey that evolves over time. Be flexible and adaptable, as the needs of your aging parents may change. Stay informed about available resources and services and be willing to adjust your caregiving approach as necessary.

Finally, know that your efforts as a caregiver are invaluable and deeply appreciated. Your love, compassion, and dedication make a significant difference in the lives of your aging parents.

Cherish the moments of connection and find strength in the knowledge that you are providing the best possible care for your loved ones.

In closing, as a Generation X caregiver, you have embarked on a remarkable journey of love and caregiving. Embrace the challenges, seek support, and find joy in the moments of connection and growth. Your role as a caregiver is a testament to the strength and compassion within you. May you find resilience, fulfillment, and peace as you navigate this caregiving journey.

Thrive Daily,

Michael Lattimore

Here is a list of relevant high-quality keywords for caregivers:

1. Caregiving for aging parents
2. Generation X caregivers
3. Elder care support
4. End-of-life planning
5. Palliative care options
6. Hospice care services
7. Grief and bereavement support
8. Assistive technologies for seniors
9. Telehealth and remote monitoring
10. Mobile apps for caregivers
11. Ethical considerations in caregiving
12. Privacy in technology use
13. Self-care for caregivers
14. Healthcare resources for aging parents
15. Legal and financial considerations in caregiving

Here's my list of relevant hashtags and keywords for caregivers:

1. #Caregiving
2. #GenerationXCaregivers
3. #AgingParents
4. #ElderCare
5. #Healthcare
6. #Wellbeing
7. #Support
8. #SelfCare
9. #EndOfLifePlanning
10. #PalliativeCare
11. #HospiceCare
12. #GriefSupport
13. #AssistiveTechnologies
14. #Telehealth
15. #RemoteMonitoring
16. #MobileApps
17. #DigitalTools
18. #EthicalConsiderations
19. #Privacy
20. #Resilience
21. MPULSE NEMT Homecare
22. Generation X caregivers
23. Person-centered support
24. Aging parents
25. Caregiving services
26. Homecare solutions

27. Elder care support
28. Empowering caregivers
29. NEMT (Non-Emergency Medical Transportation)
30. Senior care services
31. Person-centered care
32. Support for aging adults
33. Caregiver resources
34. Homecare assistance
35. Caregiving solutions

Here's a list of relevant hashtags:

1. #MPULSENEMTHomecare
2. #GenerationXCaregivers
3. #PersonCenteredSupport
4. #AgingParents
5. #CaregivingServices
6. #HomecareSolutions
7. #ElderCareSupport
8. #EmpoweringCaregivers
9. #NEMT
10. #SeniorCareServices
11. #PersonCenteredCare
12. #SupportForAgingAdults
13. #CaregiverResources
14. #HomecareAssistance
15. #CaregivingSolution

These hashtags and keywords can be used in social media posts, blog articles, or online discussions to connect with others in the caregiving community, share valuable information, and raise awareness about important caregiving topics.

GLOSSARY OF TERMS

Generation X: Thriving as Caregiver for Aging Parents

It is important to note that the definitions provided here are general and may vary depending on the context and specific sources.

1. Generation X: Refers to the generation of individuals born between the early 1960s and early 1980s. This term is often used to describe the cohort following the Baby Boomers and preceding the Millennials.
2. Person-Centered Care: An approach to healthcare that prioritizes the individual needs, preferences, and values of patients. It emphasizes collaboration, respect, and empowerment, aiming to provide care that is tailored to the unique circumstances and goals of each person.
3. Aging Parent: Refers to a parent who is advancing in age and may require additional support or care due to the physical, cognitive, or emotional changes associated with aging.
4. Caregiver: An individual who provides assistance, support, and care to another person who may have physical, cognitive, or emotional needs. In the context of this book, it refers to those who care for their aging parents.

5. End-of-Life Planning: The process of making decisions and arrangements for medical care, legal matters, and personal preferences as one approaches the end of their life. It involves discussions about advance directives, funeral arrangements, and other aspects related to the end of life.

6. Palliative Care: A specialized medical care approach that focuses on providing relief from symptoms and improving the quality of life for individuals with serious illnesses. It aims to address physical, emotional, and spiritual needs, and can be provided alongside curative treatments.

7. Hospice Care: A type of palliative care specifically designed for individuals with a life expectancy of six months or less. Hospice care focuses on providing comfort, pain management, and emotional support to individuals in the final stages of life.

8. NEMT (Non-Emergency Medical Transportation): Transportation services specifically designed to assist individuals who have difficulty accessing transportation on their own, particularly for medical appointments or healthcare-related destinations.

9. Telehealth: The use of technology, such as video conferencing or remote monitoring, to provide healthcare services remotely. It allows patients to consult with healthcare professionals, receive diagnoses, and access medical advice without physically visiting a healthcare facility.

10. Remote Monitoring: The use of technology to collect and transmit health data from individuals in their own homes or other remote locations. It enables healthcare providers to monitor vital signs, track health conditions, and provide timely interventions.

11. Nurse Case Manager: A healthcare professional who specializes in coordinating and managing the care of patients within a healthcare system. Nurse case managers work collaboratively with patients, families, healthcare providers, and insurance companies to ensure the delivery of high- quality, cost-effective, and patient-centered care.

12. Long-Term Care: Services and support provided to individuals who have chronic illnesses, disabilities, or other conditions that limit their ability to perform daily activities independently. Long- term care can be provided in various settings, including nursing homes, assisted living facilities, or in the individual's own home.

13. Care Plan: A personalized document that outlines the specific care needs, goals, and preferences of an individual. It serves as a roadmap for caregivers and healthcare professionals to ensure that the person's needs are met effectively and consistently.

14. Respite Care: Temporary care provided to relieve primary caregivers from their caregiving responsibilities. Respite care allows caregivers to take breaks, attend to their own needs, or simply recharge, while ensuring that their loved ones receive appropriate care and support.

15. Advance Directives: Legal documents that allow individuals to express their healthcare preferences and decisions in advance in case they become unable to communicate or make decisions for themselves. Examples include living wills, durable power of attorney for healthcare, and do-not-resuscitate (DNR) orders.

16. Geriatric Assessment: A comprehensive evaluation of an older adult's physical, mental, and functional well-being. It involves assessing medical history, cognitive function, physical abilities, social support, and other factors to develop a holistic understanding of the individual's health and care needs.

17. Dementia: A general term for a decline in cognitive abilities, including memory loss, impaired thinking, and difficulty with daily activities. Dementia is often caused by underlying conditions such as Alzheimer's disease, and it requires specialized care and support.

18. Care Transition: The process of moving an individual from one healthcare setting to another, such as from a hospital to a rehabilitation facility or from a nursing home to home care. Effective care transitions involve coordination, communication, and ensuring continuity of care.

19. Caregiver Burnout: Physical, mental, and emotional exhaustion experienced by caregivers due to the demands and stress of providing care. Caregiver burnout can result in decreased wellbeing and negatively impact the quality of care provided.

20. Support Groups: Gatherings of individuals who share similar experiences or challenges, providing a platform for mutual support, information sharing, and emotional connection. Caregiver support groups offer a space for caregivers to share their experiences, learn from others, and receive support from individuals who understand their unique circumstances.

21. Activities of Daily Living (ADLs): Basic self-care tasks that individuals typically perform daily, including bathing, dressing, eating, toilcting, transferring (e.g., getting in and out of bed), and maintaining continence. ADLs are often used as a measure of an individual's functional independence and can be affected by aging or health conditions.

22. Instrumental Activities of Daily Living (IADLs): More complex tasks that are necessary for independent living, such as managing finances, meal preparation, housekeeping, transportation, medication management, and using technology. IADLs require higher cognitive and organizational skills and can be challenging for individuals with cognitive impairments or physical limitations.

23. Caregiver Support Services: Programs and resources designed to help, education, and support to caregivers. These services may include counseling, respite care, support groups, educational workshops, and access to community resources.

24. Caregiver Stress: The physical, emotional, and psychological strain experienced by caregivers due to the demands and responsibilities of caregiving. Caregiver stress can manifest as fatigue, anxiety, depression, sleep disturbances, and other health issues.

25. Home Modifications: Adaptations made to a home environment to enhance safety, accessibility, and independence for individuals with mobility or functional limitations. Examples include installing grab bars, ramps, stairlifts, and bathroom modifications.

26. Care Coordination: The process of organizing and coordinating various aspects of care for an individual, involving multiple healthcare providers, services, and resources. Care coordination aims to ensure that all aspects of care are integrated, communicated effectively, and aligned with the individual's needs and goals.

27. Gerontechnology: The use of technology specifically designed for older adults to enhance their quality of life, independence, and well-being. This can include devices such as wearable health trackers, smart home systems, medication reminders, and assistive technologies.

28. Elder Abuse: The mistreatment, neglect, or exploitation of older adults, often by caregivers or family members. Elder abuse can take various forms, including physical, emotional, financial, or sexual abuse, as well as neglect or abandonment.

29. Caregiver Self-Care: The practice of taking care of one's own physical, emotional, and mental well-being as a caregiver. This includes engaging in activities that promote relaxation, stress reduction, and personal fulfillment, as well as seeking support and respite when needed.

30. Geriatric Medicine: A specialized branch of medicine that focuses on the healthcare needs of older adults. Geriatric medicine addresses the unique medical, social, and psychological aspects of aging, including the prevention, diagnosis, and management of age-related conditions and diseases.

31. Cognitive Impairment: A broad term that encompasses various conditions affecting cognitive function, such as memory loss, difficulty with thinking, problem-solving, and decision-making. Cognitive impairments can range from mild cognitive impairment (MCI) to more severe conditions like dementia or Alzheimer's disease.

32. Caregiver Training: Programs and resources that provide education and training to caregivers, equipping them with the knowledge and skills necessary to provide effective care. Caregiver training may cover topics such as medication management, communication techniques, safety precautions, and self-care strategies.

33. Geriatric Assessment Team: A multidisciplinary team of healthcare professionals specializing in geriatric care. This team typically includes geriatricians, nurses, social workers, occupational therapists, and other specialists who collaborate to assess and address the comprehensive needs of older adults.

34. Caregiver Resilience: The ability of caregivers to adapt, cope, and bounce back from the challenges and stressors of caregiving. Caregiver resilience involves developing effective coping strategies, seeking support, and maintaining a positive mindset.

35. Caregiver Advocacy: The act of speaking up and advocating for the rights, needs, and well-being of caregivers and the individuals they care for. Caregiver advocacy can involve raising awareness, influencing policies, and promoting changes that support and recognize the vital role of caregivers.

36. Geriatric Social Worker: A social worker specializing in gerontology who provides support, counseling, and assistance to older adults and their families. Geriatric social workers help navigate healthcare systems, connect individuals with community resources, and address social and emotional needs.

37. Caregiver Burden: The physical, emotional, and financial strain experienced by caregivers due to the demands and responsibilities of caregiving. Caregiver burden can result from the challenges of balancing caregiving with other responsibilities and can impact the caregiver's overall well-being.

38. Aging in Place: The ability for individuals to remain living in their own homes and communities as they age, with access to necessary support services and modifications to accommodate changing needs.

39. Geriatric Psychiatry: A specialized field of psychiatry that focuses on the mental health and well- being of older adults. Geriatric psychiatrists diagnose and treat mental health conditions that are common in older adults, such as depression, anxiety, dementia-related behavioral changes, and late-life psychosis.

40. Caregiver Support Helpline: A dedicated phone line or helpline that provides information, resources, and emotional support to caregivers. Caregiver support helplines are staffed by trained professionals who can offer guidance, answer questions, and provide referrals to relevant services.

41. Geriatric Care Manager: A professional who specializes in assessing, planning, coordinating, and monitoring the care needs of older adults. Geriatric care managers help individuals, and their families navigate the complexities of healthcare, long-term care options, and community resources.

42. Resilient Aging: The ability to adapt, maintain well-being, and thrive in the face of challenges and changes associated with aging. Resilient aging involves maintaining physical health, cognitive function, social connections, and emotional wellbeing.

43. Caregiver Empowerment: The process of equipping caregivers with the knowledge, skills, and resources necessary to provide care confidently and effectively. Caregiver empowerment involves education, support, and access to services that enhance the caregiver's ability to meet the needs of their loved ones.

44. Gerontechnologist: An expert in the field of gerontechnology who specializes in the development, implementation, and evaluation of technological solutions for older adults. Gerontechnologists work to create innovative technologies that address the unique needs and challenges of aging populations.

45. Caregiver Well-being: The overall physical, emotional, and mental health of caregivers. Caregiver well-being encompasses self-care practices, stress management, maintaining social connections, and seeking support to prevent burnout and promote a healthy caregiver experience.

46. Geriatric Rehabilitation: A specialized form of rehabilitation that focuses on restoring and maintaining functional abilities in older adults. Geriatric rehabilitation may address mobility, strength, balance, and cognitive impairments to improve independence and quality of life.

47. Caregiver Education: Programs and resources that provide caregivers with information, skills, and strategies to effectively care for their loved ones. Caregiver education may cover topics such as disease management, medication administration, communication techniques, and self-care practices.

48. Geriatric Dentistry: A branch of dentistry that focuses on the oral health needs of older adults. Geriatric dentists are trained to address age-related oral health issues, such as tooth loss, gum disease, dry mouth, and oral complications associated with chronic conditions.

49. Caregiver Support Programs: Structured programs that provide assistance, resources, and support to caregivers. These programs may include counseling, educational workshops, support groups, respite care, and access to community services.

50. Geriatric Nutrition: The study and practice of nutrition specifically tailored to the needs of older adults. Geriatric nutrition focuses on promoting healthy eating habits, addressing age-related changes in metabolism and nutrient absorption, and managing nutrition-related conditions.

51. Caregiver Fatigue: Extreme tiredness, both physical and emotional, experienced by caregivers due to the demands and responsibilities of caregiving. Caregiver fatigue can result from prolonged stress, lack of sleep, and neglecting one's own needs.

52. Geriatric Pharmacy: A specialized field of pharmacy that focuses on the medication management and optimization of drug therapy for older adults. Geriatric pharmacists work to ensure safe and effective medication use, considering factors such as age-related changes in metabolism, potential drug interactions, and medication adherence.

53. Caregiver Support Organizations: Non-profit organizations and associations that provide resources, advocacy, and support to caregivers. These organizations may offer educational materials, online forums, helplines, and local support groups.

54. Geriatric Rehabilitation: A specialized form of rehabilitation that focuses on restoring and maintaining functional abilities in older adults. Geriatric rehabilitation may address mobility, strength, balance, and cognitive impairments to improve independence and quality of life.

55. Caregiver Stress Management: Strategies and techniques aimed at reducing and managing stress experienced by caregivers. Stress management techniques may include relaxation exercises, mindfulness practices, physical activity, and seeking support from others.

56. Geriatric Oncology: A specialized field of oncology that focuses on the diagnosis, treatment, and management of cancer in older adults. Geriatric oncologists consider factors such as age-related changes in physiology, comorbidities, and functional status when developing treatment plans.

57. Caregiver Support Apps: Mobile applications designed to provide information, resources, and support to caregivers. These apps may offer features such as medication reminders, caregiver forums, stress management tools, and access to local resources.